THE ADSENSE CODE

2nd Edition

A STRATEGY

JOEL COMM

WHAT GOOGLE NEVER TOLD YOU
ABOUT MAKING MONEY WITH ADSENSE

NEW YORK

THE ADSENSE CODE
A STRATEGY
WHAT GOOGLE NEVER TOLD YOU
ABOUT MAKING MONEY WITH ADSENSE
2ND EDITION

by JOEL COMM

© 2006, 2nd Edition © 2010 Joel Comm. All rights reserved.

ISBN: 978-1-60037-706-8 (Paperback)

Published by:

Morgan James Publishing, LLC
1225 Franklin Ave. Ste 325
Garden City, NY 11530-1693
Toll Free 800-485-4943
www.MorganJamesPublishing.com

In an effort to support local communities, raise awareness and funds, Morgan James Publishing donates one percent of all book sales for the life of each book to Habitat for Humanity. Get involved today, visit
www.HelpHabitatForHumanity.org.

LEGALESE

*This book is dedicated to my wonderful family —
My beautiful wife, Mary, whom I have the privilege
of sharing my life with, Zach, my creative and
brilliant son, Jenna, who brightens any room she
walks into, and our dog, Socrates, whose furry
face and playful spirit bring joy to our home.*

INDEX

PART 1   GETTING STARTED WITH GOOGLE ADSENSE

PART 2 BEYOND BASIC ADS

PART 3   FOLLOWING THE FIGURES

PART 4   ADVANCED TOOLS AND TECHNIQUES

PART 4   QUICK TIPS

LETTER FROM THE AUTHOR

Dear Friend…

Thank you for purchasing your copy of "The AdSense Code"!

This is the latest edition of a book that has become the world's most read guide to Google AdSense. The first edition was an ebook that came out in January 2005 and was just 66 pages. Much has happened since that time and I am pleased to say that this updated edition of *The AdSense Code* is over 340 pages!

I write like I speak. I like to keep things simple so that anyone can apply what I teach quickly and easily. However, if you are new to AdSense, you might want to check out Google's <u>AdSense Support Pages</u> or occasionally refer to their online <u>Glossary</u>.

I have tried to keep this book concise and very focused on the objective of increasing your AdSense income. In this book you will find hands-on solutions to many of the concerns and challenges faced by content publishers in their quest to **attract targeted traffic**, **improve content relevance** and **increase responsiveness to AdSense ads** — using easy and legitimate techniques that have worked for me and many others.

No matter what type of website you have or the nature of your content, you will find hands-on ways to increase your AdSense income.

Through the pages of this book, I will teach you the exact-same techniques that I used to create a generous passive income with Google AdSense. These are techniques that you can apply yourself and see real results.

To those of you expecting a fat Dummies-style book with entire chapters devoted to "What the heck is AdSense?" or "A brief history of contextual advertising" this book might come as a bit of a surprise. But there's a reason for that. And the reason is that I don't want to lose you before you get to the real meaty parts. I will disclose my proven step-by-step techniques to increase your AdSense click through rate.

Isn't that the real reason you bought this book? If so, you won't be disappointed.

I don't want to hide these golden nuggets of wisdom under piles of fluff that you can read for free on the Internet. In fact, if you want to brush up on the basics, there's nothing like Google's own quick guide to AdSense. You may also find some of the material in this book repeated on various web sites and forums. I find it interesting when people tell me that this material is available at other places, because I know where many of those sites got their information in the first place!

If you are just getting started with AdSense, there is a short section at the beginning. If you don't have a website, I'll tell you how to build one, get it online and start earning with AdSense fast.

If you're already online and using AdSense — but want to know how to use it to earn much, much more — you can just skip straight past those pages and dive right into the gold! That's because getting set up with Google AdSense is the easy part. The harder part is making real money with it. And that's where this book comes in!

You'll also find some chapters on search engine optimization, traffic acquisition, content writing, ad formats and a whole host of other useful techniques that you can implement right away.

In this edition, you'll also find more information about rich media ads, strategies for combining AdSense with other advertising programs, and most importantly, combining an AdSense-optimized site with social media, perhaps now the most powerful marketing tool on the Web.

I guarantee you will find insights here that you wouldn't find any-where else.

My AdSense story — right from the sluggish $3/day times to the explosive $500/day — when AdSense pays off my mortgage, car payment, cable (and a whole lot more actually)… has taught me a great deal about how to make my web pages more profitable. And even though I have been using AdSense since 2004, my income continues to stay at these very profitable levels.

Every page is bursting with AdSense tips, tricks and proven strategies — gleaned from successful publishers who have very generously shared their money-making ideas with me.

Read. Apply. And don't forget to report your results!

Send me your comments and ask your questions if you like at www.AskJoelComm.com. I can't answer every question, but I do like to hear your success stories! Your unique problems and real-life results will help subsequent editions stay current and useful. I appreciate your input!

Joel Comm

INTRODUCTION

How To Make More Money With Google AdSense

Google wants a slice of your traffic. And it's willing to pay big bucks!

For those who have been complaining of high traffic and low sales, there's simply no better way to cash in on those hard-earned visitors to your Web pages.

AdSense makes it so easy!

There's no complicated software to install, no need to scout for affiliates, nothing to buy and no need to even have a merchant account. So…

Why isn't everybody doing this? More importantly, why isn't everybody making the most of it?

It's "Hidden Money"

"Seeing is believing", they say. Most webmasters love to obsessively track their visitors, earnings and clickthrough rates (CTR) several times a day. They love to see what's there, but they often miss what can be.

AdSense doesn't give you ultimate control over which ads are served, how the ads are rotated or what each click is worth. That's a good thing, because it's hands-free income. (It does give you some control though, and I'll tell you how to use those controls in this book.)

But many webmasters still think that once you've stuck the AdSense code on your page, there's little you can do except wait and watch.

Nothing could be further from the truth! Google gives you a great deal of control over your ads, and especially their visual or graphic elements. By tweaking these elements to your advantage, you could easily — in as little as a few minutes — multiply your clickthroughs many, many times over!

My Experiments with AdSense

I signed up with AdSense in June 2003, starting small by serving AdSense off just a few of my pages.

By the end of the day, I'd delivered several thousand AdSense impressions — which netted me the princely sum of… $3.00. I didn't exactly burn down the house.

While I didn't see a great deal of potential based on this initial figure, I figured it couldn't hurt to place AdSense code on more pages. Over the period of a couple months, I increased my impressions 25-fold, but the clicks just weren't happening. That was when I hit my lowest point as an Internet publisher. My clickthrough ratios were so bad, I needed thousands of visitors to net about $30 per day.

At that point, I knew something had to change — and I was going to change it!

It was as late as April 2004 — ten months after I signed up with AdSense — that I had my eyes opened to what I had been missing all along. It was one of the "Ah-Ha!" moments where I felt as though I was being hit by the proverbial two-by-four. Immediately, I began experimenting with my Google ads, testing various placement and colors to see if my assumptions would hold water.

The results were fast — and fantastic!

By applying the same easy tweaks discussed in this book, I nearly tripled my clickthrough rate, and my income shot up to $600 PER DAY! I still remember that golden day in April 2004 — and for me there's been no looking back.

From my early days of being an "AdSense nobody" to becoming a leading AdSense and Internet marketing guru, when a five-figure monthly income no longer surprises me… it's been an eventful journey full of learning experiences.

Little cogs run the AdSense machinery!

It's easy to get carried away when you're making so much money. But I never lose sight of the little things that make me big money with AdSense.Every AdSense partner — however big or small — knows that at the end of the day, it all boils down to one thing: stats! Your AdSense stats might not be amazing to start with, but make it a habit to go through it with a fine-toothed comb. As you start making sense of those 'little numbers'… the big checks will follow!

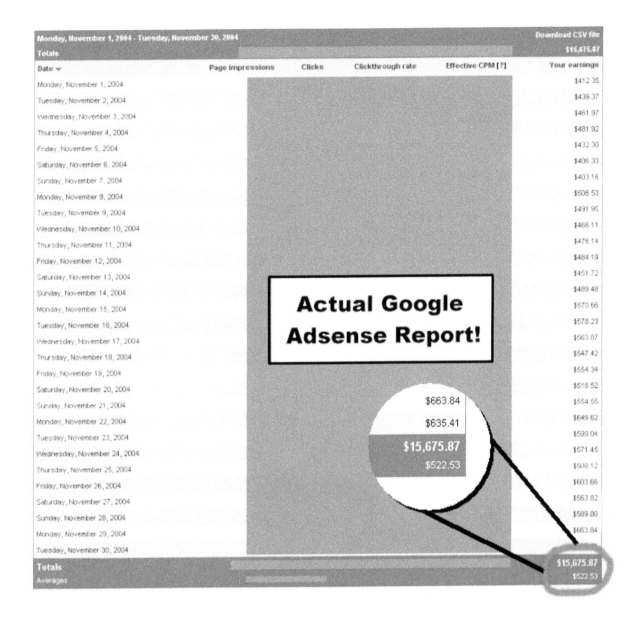

Stats are the holy grail of Internet Marketing. This is a real screenshot of my AdSense stats page taken way back in 2004. You can see what I was making daily then—and believe me, I'm making much more now—but specific details such as CPM and CTR have been blacked out in keeping with Google's terms of service.

Hitting the AdSense Jackpot!

As you can see, AdSense can easily take care of my car payment, mortgage, cable bills and a whole lot more besides.

Aren't you dying to know...

WHAT was it I did to AdSense — and my website — that turned it overnight into a cash-cow on steroids?!

More importantly, what can YOU do to shoot your AdSense income through the roof- right NOW!

My advice to you is quite simple...

Don't be passive about your AdSense income; work hard to increase it. But before you try out that hot new idea you read about at an Internet Forum, be sure to check out Google's AdSense TOS. Some web publishers have forever relinquished their fat AdSense paychecks, just because they were too busy to pay attention to something so fundamental to their AdSense survival.

I like to play by the rules and have taken adequate care to ensure that my AdSense tips and tweaks are legit. Making what I do from AdSense, I have little incentive to go on a rule-breaking spree and get my AdSense account suspended.

For many Internet site owners, AdSense is like the goose that lays the golden egg. Take good care of your goose — don't slaughter it in the mad rush to increase your AdSense income!

Part
1

Getting Started With
Google Adsense

1. GETTING STARTED WITH GOOGLE ADSENSE

1.1 The Basics: Building Your Site

Since the first edition of this book came out lots of people started asking me how they can make money with AdSense. I'm always happy to help people make the most of Google, but many of these people didn't even have a website!

Here's the bad news: to make money with AdSense, you've got to have a website. There's no getting around that. The good news though is that it's never been easier to create a website from scratch and use it to generate real revenue.

I'm going to give a brief introduction here to creating a website from the ground up. You can find plenty more information online and I'll tell you where to look. A good place to start is my own book How To Build Profitable Websites Fast, available at www.buildawebsitefast.com.

If you already have a site up and running, you can just skip this bit, head down to 1.10 and begin reading about how to improve your AdSense revenues.

1.2 Naming and Hosting Your Site

The first thing your site will need is a name. That's easier said than done these days. All the best words in the dictionary have either already been bought and built by developers or they've been bought and offered by speculators.

But that doesn't mean you can't create a good name and buy it for a song. Putting two words together with a hyphen can work (like www.adsense-secrets.com) and there are plenty of good names available if you're prepared to move outside the world of .coms into .net and .biz etc.

Your site is going to be stored on a hosting company's server. (You didn't want thousands of people dialing into your computer every hour, did you?) Again, there are lots of different options available depending on how much you want to pay and what you need.

Your first stop to solve both the domain name and hosting should be Host Gator. (www.DomainAnything. com) This is a nuts and bolts service that lets you hunt and buy names, order hosting plans and even submit your site to the search engines. When you're looking for a name, you can just toss in ten options and the site will tell you which (if any) are available. Buying a name won't cost you more than about $9 a year. Hosting shouldn't cost more than $10/month, and that will cover everything you will need to get started.

If you can't find a name you like and that hasn't already been grabbed, you can take a look at sites like www.moderndomains.com and www.bestnames.net. These are companies that buy domain names and sell them for a profit. There's a good chance you'll find some good names here but they can cost you anything from $50 to $50,000. Before you part with a penny, think about the advantage that a good name can bring and ask yourself if you can't get the extra traffic a cheaper way. Often, you can.

1.3 Designing The Site

It used to be said that absolutely anyone could create a website. That was true: absolutely anyone who knew HTML. Today, you don't even need to know that. Programs like Microsoft's FrontPage or NVU (which is free; you can download it at www.nvu.com) let you create sites without you needing to know your tags from your tables. You can also try Joomla, a content management system which is downloadable for free from www.joomla.com. Once you've downloaded it, you'll just need to upload it and install it on your server. There are plenty of templates available that you can then purchase or find for free. In short, if you can use Word, you can create a website.

You can either have fun playing with the programs and designing the site yourself or you can hire a professional designer to do it for you.

Freelance sites like www.elance.com and www.guru.com are good places to advertise. You can invite designers to give you quotes and pick the best based on price and talent. Be sure to check feedback and portfolios though; a low bid is often low for a good reason.

1.4 Creating Content

In Chapter 11, I talk in detail about building content and optimizing what you write to attract traffic and maximize your AdSense revenues. There are all sorts of ways to do that but for the moment just bear in mind that the ads that appear on your site will depend on the content on your pages. That's how AdSense works: users click on the ads because they're relevant.

And that's why it's not worth putting up a site just to cash in on particular keywords. Google doesn't like it and neither do users. If your site doesn't genuinely interest your visitors, you'll find it hard to get traffic, links and clicks on your ads.

But there are still a lot of different ways to create content very easily that improves your income. I'll tell you all about them in chapter 11.

It's also worth remembering that Google doesn't place ads on particular types of sites, so if you're thinking of building a casino site stuffed with AdSense ads, you can forget about it; it's not going to happen.

Before you build a site that contains any content that's remotely controversial, check out the AdSense Terms of Service (TOS) to make sure that it's allowed. It will tell you whether your idea is sound or whether you need to think again.

1.5 Getting Started With Blogger.com...

Want to get up and running with AdSense really fast? One way is to open an account at Blogger.com.

Blogger is like those old free websites that you could set up in a flash but which looked like they'd been cobbled together from bits of left-over graphics that no one else wanted. Except that the blog you create at Blogger.com is the real McCoy. It's professional, it looks great... and it takes just seconds to put together.

All you have to do is choose a name and title for your blog, take your pick of the good range of templates available and get writing.

You don't have to worry about coding or design work or images or anything else. If you change your mind about the way your blog looks, you can just pick a different template. All that's left for you to do is write... and add AdSense.

Even that's been made easy for you.

Because Blogger.com is now owned by Google, you can apply for AdSense directly from its site. It even gives you a preview of where your ads will appear and how they will look. While you're waiting for your approval, you can play with fonts and colors so that you're all set up and ready to start earning.

Of course, once you've done that, there are all sorts of ways to play with the layout and content. You can easily move the ads into the sidebar by clicking the Template tab and looking for the line that says:

<!-- Begin #sidebar -->

<div id="sidebar"><div id="sidebar2">

Just paste the AdSense code directly beneath it. But that's certainly not all. Later in this book, I explain lots of different, advanced strategies that you can use to maximize your AdSense earnings on your blog. You should certainly use them but more important is that you make a start.

With Blogger.com, you can do that in seconds. It's a great way to get started, but you should think of it as blogging with training wheels. After a bit you'll want to move to your own domain so you can really pick up speed!

1.6 ... Or Google's Page Creator

But blogs aren't for everyone. Although they're now one of the easiest ways to get online, they have to be updated regularly and aren't the best option for static content.

Fortunately Blogger isn't the only way to get online fast. Google's Page Creator at pages.google.com makes building a website as simple as point, click and type.

Again, you get a template that you can edit freely, and you can also break into the HTML to paste the AdSense code. Check to see how it looks, publish, and all you'll have to do next is let people know where you are.

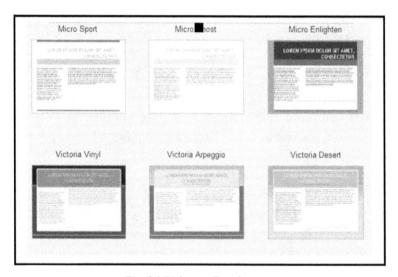

Fig. 1.1 Pick your Google page.

And that's where the disadvantages of creating a website using a free tool like Page Creator kicks in.

With a website created through Page Creator, Search Engine Optimization becomes difficult. Your URL will be [yourname].googlepages.com, which is about as catchy a ball of slush. It's unlikely to get very far in search engines and when you try to spread it around, it will simply make you look unprofessional.

Page Creator can be a useful place to get started but it's really designed to help people like teachers display information to a closed audience. It's not a good way to earn a lot of money.

If you're keen to get started though, if you have an audience already set up... or if you just want to see your stuff online fast — and with ads — then it's a fun toy to play with.

And you can always move your content onto your own URL when you're ready.

1.7 Search Engine Optimization

However you decide to build your first site, people have to know you're there. One of the most important ways to do that is get yourself a high ranking in a search engine.

There are lots of different search engines, but only three are really important: Google, Yahoo! and MSN. In chapter 22, I'll talk in more detail about improving your search engine rankings.

If you want to take a shortcut, there are plenty of companies which will make the submissions for you and they'll even optimize your site to get you as high in the rankings as possible.

1.8 Links

Your search engine ranking will depend on a number of factors. One of those factors is the number of sites that link to yours. As far as Google is concerned if lots of sites about model railways link to your model railway site, people who like model railways must think your site is good. So they'll want to offer it to people who search for model railways, bringing you lots of free traffic.

Once you've got your site up and running you'll want to persuade other sites to give you links. You could offer to exchange links and you could even set up a page that contains recommended links so that you'll have somewhere to put them.

There's a range of other strategies and services that you can use. You can find out about those in chapter 21.

2. ADSENSE — MAKING THE MONEY!

Once you've done all this, you'll be ready to start using — and profiting from — AdSense. I'm going to talk you right through the process of signing up to AdSense from reaching Google to being ready to place your first ad.

If you've been putting off signing up until you get time to figure out how to do it, you've just run out of excuses!

2.1 What Is AdSense?

Before signing up to AdSense, it's important to understand what you're signing up to. Many of the principles and strategies that I describe in this book make the most of the way that AdSense works. If you can understand where AdSense is getting its ads, how it assigns those ads to Web pages and how it fixes the prices for clicks on those ads or for ad appearances on those pages, you'll be in a great position to manipulate AdSense in a way that gives you maximum revenues.

Unfortunately, I can't really do that.

Much of the way that Google runs the AdSense program is kept under wraps. I know a few things — and enough to do a great deal with our AdSense ads. But I don't know it all. No one outside Google does. And for good reason. If it was clear how Google figured out the content of each website and which ads suit that site best, there's a good chance that the Web would be filled with sites created specially to bring in the highest paying ads instead of sites built to bring in and inform users.

People do try to build sites for ads not content, but they tend to make less money than high quality sites that attract loyal users who click on ads.

The fact is, we can make the most of both AdSense and our own ad space without knowing the algorithms that Google uses to assign ads and pay sites.

That's because AdSense is pretty simple. **At the most basic level, AdSense is a service run by Google that places ads on websites.** When you sign up to AdSense, you agree to take the ads that Google gives you and receive a fee each time a user clicks on that ad (or for each thousand ad appearances the ad receives on your site, depending on the type of ad).

The ads themselves come from another Google service: AdWords.

If you want to understand AdSense, you will need to understand AdWords.

Advertisers submit their ads to Google using the AdWords program. They write a headline and a short piece of text — and here's where it gets interesting — they choose how much they want to pay.

Advertisers decide on the size of their advertising budgets and the amount they're prepared to pay for each click they receive. Google then decides where to put those ads.

So a company that has a website selling handmade furniture might create an ad that looks like this:

> Handmade furnishings
> From baby cribs to walnut
> bookcases, we do it all.
> Traditional quality, low prices.
> www.handmadefurnishings.com

The company's owner might then say that he's prepared to pay $1000 a month for his advertising budget but not more than $1 for a click. He can be certain now of getting at least a thousand leads a month.

But that's usually where his control over the ad ends. Google will figure out which sites suit an ad like that and put them where it sees fit, charging the advertiser up to a dollar a click until the advertiser's budget runs out. (Of that dollar, how much the publisher receives is a Google secret. *The New York Times* has reported Google pays publishers 78.5 percent of the advertising price per click. The figure hasn't been confirmed but it is around what most people in the industry expect that Google pays.)

That makes AdWords different to more traditional form of advertising. In the print world, an advertiser chooses where it wants to place its ads and decides if the price is worth paying.

The newspaper too decides how much it wants advertisers to pay to appear on its pages. Any advertiser that meets that price gets the slot and the publisher always knows how much his space is worth.

Neither of those things is usually true online. I say "usually" because Google does now allow advertisers to place their ads on selected websites and even on selected spots on those sites. They still have to outbid other ads that are eligible to appear on those pages though, so there's no guarantee the placement will be successful. The vast majority of advertisers leave it to Google to decide where to put their ads.

The result is that when an advertiser signs up to AdWords, he has no idea where his ads are going to turn up. **When you sign up to AdSense, you've got no idea how much you're going to be paid for the ad space on your page or which ads are going to appear there.**

You leave it to Google to decide whether to give you ads which could pay just a few cents per click or ads which could pay a few dollars per click.

Google says that it always assigns ads in such a way that publishers receive maximum revenues, and that advertisers get the best value for their money.

So if you have a site that talks about interior design and which mentions "homemade furnishings" a great deal, Google will assume that your readers will be interested in the sample ad. But that won't be the only ad that could appear on your page. There could be dozens of others. Google will give you the ads that it thinks will give you the highest revenues.

That might not be the ad with the highest possible click price though. If a lower paying ad gives you more clicks and higher overall revenues, you should find yourself receiving that ad instead.

In theory then, you could just leave it to Google to decide which ads to give you and at which price.

In my experience though, that just cuts you out of a giant opportunity. You *can* influence the choice of ads that you get on your page, both in terms of content and in terms of price. You can certainly influence the number of clicks you receive on those ads. Google leaves that entirely up to you — and it's a crucial part of the difference between earnings that pay for candy bars and earnings that pay for cars.

In short then, while signing up for AdSense can be both the beginning and the end of turning your site into income, if you're serious about making serious money with your site, it needs to be the beginning. You'll want to make sure you're not getting low-paying ads, and you'll want to make sure that you're getting the clicks that turn those ads into cash.

If you want an in-depth look at Google AdWords, I recommend Perry Marshall's training materials at www.perrymarshall.com.

2.2 Signing Up Made Easy

First though, you have to sign up to AdSense. Here's how you do it.

The sign-up page asks for a relatively small amount of information, not all of which is as obvious as you might like.

First, you'll have to tell Google whether you want an "individual" account or a "company" account — whether you're a company with more than twenty employees or practically a one-man show that's just you and up to nineteen others. That's important for just one reason: it tells Google where to send the money. Take a business account and the payments will be made in the name of your company; take an individual account, and they'll be paid directly to you.

You'll also be able to choose between three different ways of receiving your money: Electronic Funds Transfer, local currency check or Secured Express Delivery. **In general, it's better to get your money by direct deposit using the Electronic Funds Transfer; Google charges for express mail checks.**

(What you won't be able to choose is whether you're paid on a cost-per-click (CPC) basis, or on a cost per mille (CPM) basis that pays for every thousand times you show an ad. Google decides that for you. Some ads will be CPC and others will be CPM.)

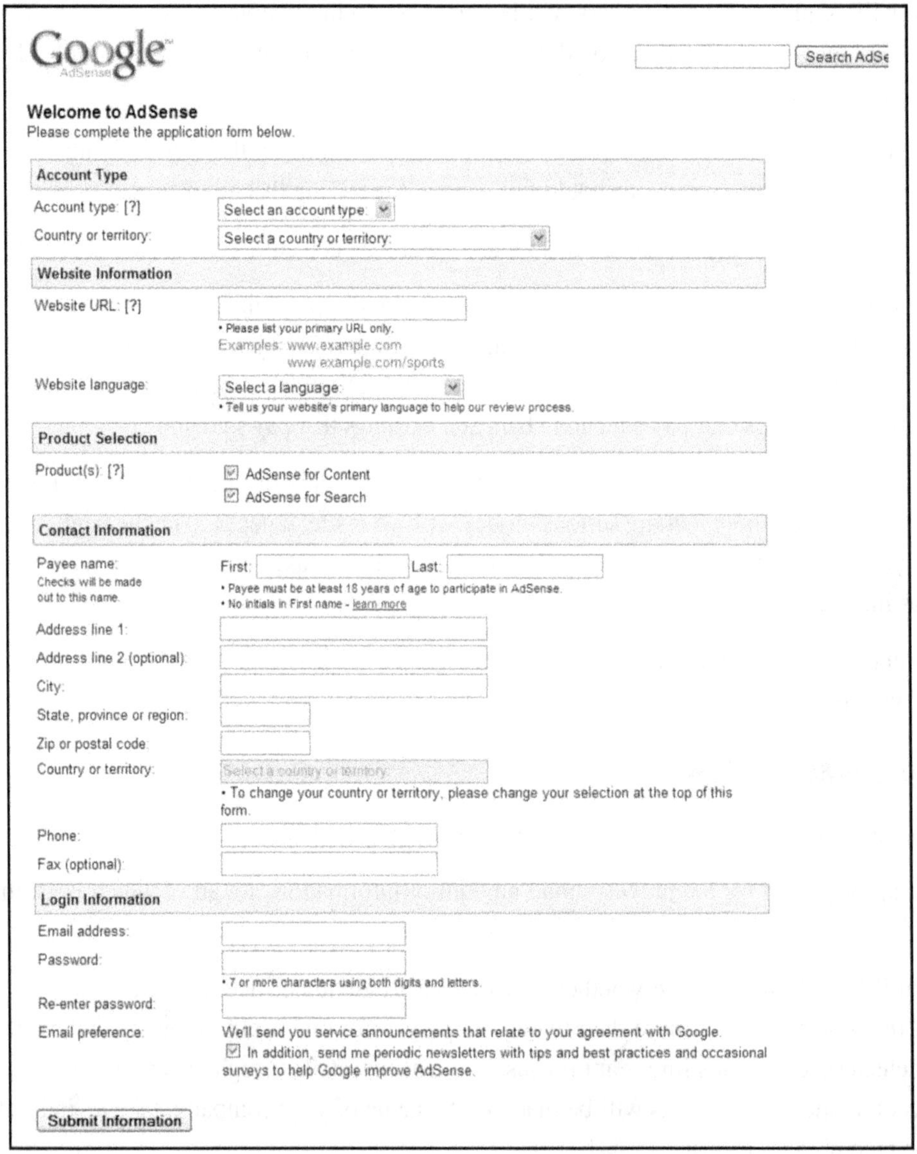

Fig. 2.1 The AdSense sign up page

The next piece of information that Google demands is your URL. There's only room for one URL, which can be confusing if you have more than one site and want to put AdSense on all of them. Don't worry about it. It won't affect how you use AdSense at all, so just submit your biggest site for now.

Once you're approved, you'll just have to copy and paste a small piece of code into your website and you're done!

2.3 Google Policies

AdSense works. I know it works because I've got the stats, the checks and the bank balance to prove it. And all of the methods that I used to increase my AdSense revenues were completely legitimate and in line with Google's policies.

That's important. It is possible to cheat AdSense. But you'd have to be crazy to do it. You can make so much money working within Google's rules that to risk getting thrown out by putting ads on pages without content or by persuading users to click on the ads is just plain crazy.

I've put a detailed list of Google's "do's and don'ts" at the back of this book. The things to look out for in particular are:

Code Modification

You have to paste the AdSense code onto your site as is. And you don't need to do anything else! Your AdSense account will let you play with colors and placements (and getting those right is what will really rocket your income) so why bother playing with Google's HTML? It's not necessary and it could get you a lifetime ban.

Incentives

When the ads appear on your page, you have to leave them completely alone. You might be tempted to tell your users to "click here" or support your sponsors but if Google catches you, they could well cut you off. They want people to click because they're genuinely interested in the ad. Get your strategy right and they'll do just that.

You <u>can</u> encourage your users to download the products your affiliate links promote or to use your search bar, but <u>never</u> encourage your users to click your ads.

Content

Google is pretty picky about where the ads are displayed. They don't want advertisers complaining to them that their services were being promoted on a site that supports gambling or is filled with profanity or contains more ads than content. If your content doesn't come up to scratch, you'll need a site that does.

Prohibited Clicks

And nastiest of all are the people who either click on their own ads or create programs to do it for them.

The bottom line is that you don't need any of this stuff. Maximizing your revenue *within the rules* is a breeze!

2.4 As Easy as 1-2-3!

The bottom line is that there are three ways to increase your AdSense revenue.

1. **By Tweaking the Ads**
    to make them more appealing to your visitors;

2. **By Optimizing your Website**
    for better AdSense targeting (or what the Google folks call 'content relevance');

    And the only sure-fire way to get 1 and 2 right is by

3. **Tracking Visitor Response.**

If you don't know what works (and what doesn't work) in trying to increase your AdSense revenue... you're shooting arrows in the dark!

The right tracking tools can reveal a great deal about your visitors and answer fundamental questions such as **what they're looking for** and   **what makes them 'click'**. Once you've figured that out, bingo! You're on your way to big AdSense bucks!

But it isn't as straightforward as it seems. If it were, there wouldn't be so many grumpy people on AdSense forums complaining about their low AdSense earnings.

It's not that they aren't doing anything about it. They simply aren't doing the right things.

Let me assure you that in the time that I have been using AdSense, my earnings have only gone up — and so will yours, if you apply all my techniques seriously.

3. HOW TO "TWEAK" YOUR ADS TO MAKE THEM "CLICK"!

3.1 Ad Formats: "Dress" your ads for success!

How would you like your ads served? Banners? Skyscrapers? Rectangles? Squares? What about borders and background colors?

The choices can be overwhelming. Many people let Google decide for them- preferring to stick with the default settings. Big mistake! From my own experience I can tell you that it's like swapping a hundred-dollar bill for a ten-dollar one.

For almost one year I settled for just a tenth of what I could have been making — just because I didn't bother to control the looks and placement of my AdSense ads.

The various ad formats, colors and their placement on the Web page can be done in thousands of combinations. You can literally spend hours every day experimenting with every possible combination. But you don't want to, do you?

Let me give you a few 'ground rules' that have sky-rocketed the CTRs on my top-grossing pages:

3.2 Don't "Look" Like An Ad

People don't visit your website for ads. They want good content.

If you make the ads stick out with eye-popping colors, images or borders, that makes them easy to recognize as ads — and people work extra hard to avoid them.

The same goes for ads that are tucked away in the top, bottom or some other far corner of the page. So easy to ignore!

If you want people to click, make the ads look like an integral part of your content.

> Today's visitors are blind to banners, mad at pop-ups, weary of ads and skeptical of contests and giveaways. So how do you win their confidence? Simple. Don't make your ads look like ads!

Let's begin by reviewing each of the different types of ad available from AdSense and explaining their uses... then I'll introduce you to a few simple choices that zoomed my CTRs to incredible heights.

3.3 Meet the AdSense Family

Google serves its ads in several flavors, with each of those flavors coming in a range of different shapes and sizes. It is very important to understand the differences between each of these ads. Some are ideal for particular locations. Some should never be used in certain locations. And some should be used very rarely—if at all.

The sample page at www.google.com/adsense/adformats lets you see all of the different kinds of ads at once. It even has links to sample placements that demonstrate how the ads can be used.

For the most part, I'd recommend that you ignore those sample placements.

I'll talk about location in more detail later in the book, but for now just bear in mind that many of the ads in the samples are just too out of the way to be noticed.

You can use them as a starting point if you want but you'll save yourself a lot of time — and money — by taking advantage of the experience of myself and others, and following the recommendations here.

3.4 Text Ads — Google's Finest

Text ads are probably the types of ad that you're most familiar with. You get a box containing one or a number of ads with a linked headline, a brief description and a URL. You also get the "Ads by Google" notice that appears on all AdSense ads. (Google changed this notice recently and it now blends in much better than it used to.)

There are now about twelve different types of text ad. One of the most popular is the **leaderboard**. At 728 x 90, it stretches pretty much across the screen and while it can be placed anywhere, it's mostly used at the top of the page, above the main text.

Fig. 3.1 The leaderboard.

That's a great location. It's the first thing the reader sees and it offers a good selection of ads to choose from. When you're just starting out and still experimenting with the types of ads that work best with your users, it's a pretty good default to begin with.

Of course, you can put it in other places too. Putting a leaderboard ad between forum entries for example can be a pretty good strategy sometimes and definitely worth trying. On the whole though, I think you'll probably find that one of the smaller ads, such as a banner or half-banner might blend in more there and bring better results.

And I think you can often forget about putting a leaderboard at the bottom of the page, despite what Google's samples show you. It would certainly fit there but you have to be certain that people are going to reach the bottom of the page, especially a long page. You might find that only a small minority of readers would get that far, so you're already reducing the percentage of readers who would click through.

Overall, I'd say that leaderboards are most effective blended into the top of the page beneath the navigation bar and sometimes placed between forum entries.

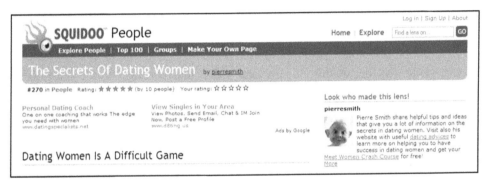

Fig. 3.2 A nicely optimized half banner on this Squidoo page.

Banners (468 x 60) and **half-banners** (234 x 60) are much more flexible.

Like leaderboards you can certainly put these sorts of ads at the top of the page, and lots of sites do it. Again, that's something worth trying. You can put up a leaderboard for a week or so, swap it for a banner for another week or so, and compare the results.

Fig. 3.3 A banner and a half-banner.

But at the top of the page, I'd expect the leaderboard to do better.

A banner or a half-banner would leave too much space on one side and make the ad stand out. It would look like you've set aside an area of the page for advertising instead of for content. That would alert the reader that that section of the page is one that they can just ignore.

When you're looking for an ad to put in the middle of the page though, a half-banner can be just the ticket.

While a leaderboard will stretch over the sidebars of your site, just like the navigation bar, a 234 x 60 half-banner will fit neatly into the text space on most sites.

This sort of ad should be your default option for the end of articles and the bottom of blog entries.

But for the most part, stay away from the 468 x 60 banner ad block!

One of the first things people do when they sign up for AdSense is to grab a 468 x 60 ad block.

Big mistake.

I have a theory about why they do this. It's the same theory that explains why the 468 x 60 block does *not* entice clicks.

Most site owners have the mindset that when they put Google ads on their site, they must place the code that conforms most to traditional web advertising. And that would be...? Yup, the 468 x 60, the ubiquitous banner format that we have all come to know and love and... IGNORE.

Everyone is familiar with the 468 x 60. And that's exactly why the clickthrough rate on this size is very low, even among advertisers who use images on their banners.

The 468 x 60 blocks screams, "Hey! I am an advertisement! Whatever you do, DON'T click me. In fact, you should run from me as fast as you can!"

In all but a few special cases, I have found the 468 x 60 ad block to be completely ineffective, and recommend ignoring it the same way your visitors do.

Now, that doesn't mean you can *never* use it. You just have to know what you're doing and do it smartly. *You have to do everything you can to make sure that that ad block looks absolutely nothing like a traditional banner ad.*

At my site, WorldVillage.com, I've done that by surrounding the ad with text. Because there's no border around the unit, the ads blend into the text and look almost as though they're a part of the article.

If I had left that unit in the middle of some empty space — at the top of the page for example — it would have looked exactly like the sort of banner that users have trained themselves to avoid. It wouldn't have picked up any clicks at all.

(Note, I could probably have used a half-banner here too but in general, I like to give my users as wide a choice of ads to click as possible.)

While this use of a 468 x 60 works for me — and it can work for you too if you blend it into the page properly — I'd stick to other formats, like the half-banner if you're not 100 percent sure that you can pull it off.

When this ad unit fails, it can fail big.

Google also offers six different kinds of rectangular ads: **buttons** (125 x 125), **small rectangles** (180 x 150), **medium rectangles** (300 x 250), **large rectangles** (336 x 280), and two sizes of **squares** 250 x 250 and 200 x 200.

In fact, all of the rectangles can be slotted into the same spots on the page... with the exception of the button.

Fig. 3.4 Banner ads at WorldVillage.com. Note how the ad links come immediately after an article link so that the ads look like part of the site.

Probably the most common use of rectangles is at the beginning of articles. You can wrap the text around the ad, forcing the reader to look at it if he wants to read the article. That's very effective.

But you can really put these sorts of ads anywhere on the page. On my site, DealOfDay.com, I've put two rectangular ads right at the top of the page so that they take up the bulk of the space the user sees before he starts to scroll. That's a very aggressive approach that might not work on every site. It's worth trying though because if it works for you, you can find that it brings in great revenues.

Fig. 3.5 Small, medium and large rectangles... and the square.

If you're wondering which size of ad would be best for the position you've got in mind, my advice is to start with the large rectangle, the 336 x 280.

Why should you choose the 336 x 280 ad block? Simple. It gets the most clicks! My studies have shown that this format looks most like real content added to a page. I've dabbled with every size Google offers and this is the size that consistently has the best results. Other people have told me the exact same thing. That's all I need to know!

Second best is the 300 x 250 rectangle.

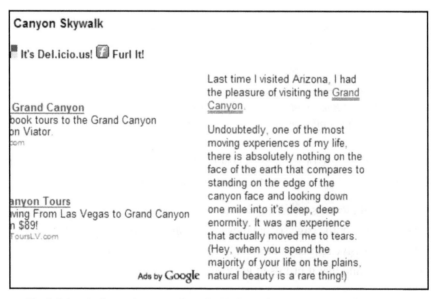

Fig. 3.6 A typical use of a rectangle embedded into the text at www.joelcomm.com...

This ad block size is really useful when you want to have two sets of ads side by side. They fit on most web pages just perfectly.

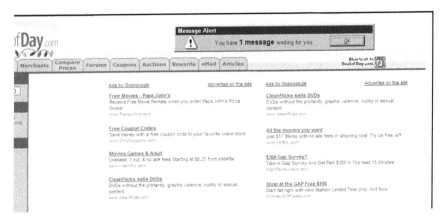

Fig. 3.7 ... and an atypical use of two rectangles at Dealofday.com.

Buttons should generally be used in a different way to other rectangles. Like the half-banners, they're distinctive for their small size. While that means you could slot them in anywhere, I think they work best when slipped into the sidebars.

For example, you might have a list of links to frequently-read articles or other sites on one side of your page. Putting a button ad at the end of a list like that could help it to blend in well.

The final types of text ads are those that run vertically. These come in three sizes: **skyscraper** (120 x 600), **wide skyscraper** (160 x 600) and **vertical banner** (120 x 240).

Clearly, these are useful options for filling up the sides of the page.

I would also recommend using the 'wide skyscraper', text-only ads on the right hand edge of the screen — in conjunction with the 3-Way Matching I discuss later in the book.

If you think about it, nearly all PC users are right handed (even left-handed people like me control their mouse with their right hand because it's how we were 'brought up' to use a mouse.) By placing the ads on the right edge it's psychologically 'less distance' between your right hand and the screen.

This 'closeness' in my opinion makes the user feel more comfortable and therefore more likely to click through to a link. They feel more in control of their visit experience.

On the whole, you can often divide sites into those that have plenty of content at the sides (especially on some blogs), and those that have nothing on the sides (like at JoelComm.com).

I think putting vertical ads in space so that they form the border of the main text makes the page look a lot cleaner. But that doesn't necessarily mean that they're going to get more clicks. If you're putting a vertical banner in an area where you have other content then just make sure, as always, that you blend them in well so that they look like the rest of your content.

3.5 Next And Previous Buttons For Browsing Ads

Google does everything it can to match ads to the content on your website. It checks your metatags, reads your titles, looks for keywords... and does a whole lot of other things that it just won't tell us about.

And for text ads that pay on a CPC basis, it now lets users browse backwards and forwards until they find ads that interest them.

In one of the bottom corners of the ad unit, there are two little arrows that users can click to generate new ads.

Fig. 3.8 "Next" arrows on an ad at WorldVillage.com. A nice idea but will people click them?

Unfortunately, you don't get paid when people click the arrows. You only get paid if people click the new ads that the arrows bring up.

But what are the odds that a user is going to bother clicking arrows to look for new ads?

I can't imagine that your site's readers are going to make much use of these arrows. They've come to your site to read your content. If they spot an ad that they find interesting, some of them will click and generate a commission for you.

But if they don't spot something that they want to read, they're going to click away.

If you're lucky, you might get a few clicks out of curiosity but I haven't noticed any significant rise in my AdSense earnings since Google introduced these arrows.

That doesn't mean I haven't found them useful though.

I can try to optimize my pages to bring in the ads I want, and there are various strategies that I can use to make sure that those ads match my content. But until the ads appear on my page, I've got no idea what sort of companies might be offering their products.

By clicking the next and previous buttons, I can get an idea of the sort of ads that might be available to me.

The ads you see first will be for products that Google considers to be of most interest to your users and which pay the highest amounts. But if you wanted to try to bring up different ads — and I'll explain how to do that later in this book — you can now see what you're aiming for.

Just make sure that you only click the next and previous buttons, and not the ads themselves!

Because you don't get paid to bring up new ads, Google shouldn't mind you clicking those arrows. Miss the arrow and hit a link though and you could find your account being shut down.

Aim your cursor carefully!

3.6 Image Ads — Built To Be Ignored

Text ads should always be your first pick when you start to load up your site. Image ads should always be your last choice.

A text ad offers many advantages over image ads:

1. With the right formatting, **a text ad 'blends in' with your site content**. An image ad will not give you the same freedom with its appearance, as the only thing you can play with is the size and positioning.

2. **You can squeeze more text ads** into the space that a conventional banner takes. People love to have more choices!

3. **Properly formatted text ads don't look like clutter**.
   Banners do!

4. **People hate banners** and avoid them at sight. Many tests confirm that people are much more receptive to text ads related with your content.

I just can't think of a reason why anyone would want to take an image ad from Google. Text ads perform so much better, in my opinion, you're better off sticking with those and ignoring image ads altogether.

I've experimented and I can tell you that these two steps (putting the ad in the middle of the content and removing any overt border colors) can at least *double* your click thru rate (or CTR) and that means that you'll be making more money with the same number of visitors. And that's a good thing.

So let's have a look at how to do this.

First off, have a look at the different ad formats. Most people seem to go with the default "banner" format ads, which is too bad: after the last few years of surfing, I think people have been trained to ignore these banner adverts. Even the spiffy new graphical banners, like this:

: how you can get creative with the placement. Also, if you're going to have an
eaders and have a layout that has at least four ads, if not five? Really, the one-ad
/e an ad at all, why not maximize the chance it'll have something of interest to your

Fig. 3.9 This banner ad stands out, but will it get clicked? Dave Taylor, best-selling technology writer and AdSense partner, stands up for text ads in this article at:
http://www.free-web-money.com/000449.html

3.7 Video Ads

There is however, one type of image ad that you should welcome on your website: Google's video ads.

These are an excellent addition to Google's inventory and for sites that get them, they can bring very impressive returns.

Instead of receiving the sort of static image that just gets ignored, you'll receive the opening still of an online video. The video is stored on Google's servers so your download times won't be affected, and it only plays when the user clicks the Play button, minimizing distraction to the user.

That's a good thing. If a user's eyes keep drifting to a moving image when he's trying to read your content, he's going to get pretty frustrated and not want to come back.

Fig. 3.10 Play-per-click: a scene from Google's sample video ad.

And it's fine too if you're being paid on a CPM basis; you won't care then how often someone sees the video. But you're not always paid on a CPM basis; you might also be paid on a CPC basis.

Unlike Google's other ad formats though, you won't be paid for just one click. Users first have to click the Play button—which won't pay you a dime—and then click either the screen while it's playing or the link underneath the screen before you'll earn money.

In fact, you can't even track the number of times the film is shown. (Although that does mean that you can watch the film yourself without getting rude messages from Google, and it also means that CPC advertisers are less likely to get free branding at the expense of your page space.)

That extra step might sound like it's going to hit your clickthrough rate for that ad unit but I'm not sure that's true.

As soon as someone sees a button anywhere, they want to click it. In fact, I'm sure that if you put a big notice next to the Play button saying, "DO NOT PUSH THIS BUTTON" you can be sure that your clicks would go through the roof. (But don't try it; it's unlikely that Google will appreciate it.)

People will want to click that Play button, and many of them will want to learn more about the company that created the ad. And even if your CTR does drop for that unit, it's likely that the click price for video ads will be higher than for other units competing for that space.

Video ads are more expensive to create than text or image ads. That's why they tend to be created by big companies like car giants or Disney. They might even be offering their television ads. If those corporations have gone to the trouble creating an original video ad or formatting a television ad for the Web, there's a great chance that they'll go to the trouble of outbidding their nearest rival for exposure.

If you're getting a video ad, track how long it appears on that page and compare the revenues it brings with the days on which no video ad appeared. You should expect to see a spike in earnings. If you don't see that spike, you can always opt out.

Unlike text or image ads though, there's no guarantee you're going to get a video ad. To qualify, you have to be opted in to receive image ads on an ad unit in one of these sizes:

- Medium Rectangle (300x250)
- Large Rectangle (336x280)
- Square (250x250)
- Small Square (200x200)
- Leaderboard (28x90)
- Skyscraper (120x600)
- Wide Skyscraper (160x600)

(It's worth noting that with video ads, the bigger the format, the better the results).

If you're receiving those kinds of image ads *and* AdSense has a video ad to match your content, you might receive one.

But what if you don't? You'll be receiving the sort of image ads that earn a poor clickthrough rate. That would cost you money.

There are two things that you can do to minimize any losses from fishing for video ads and not getting them.

The first is to stop fishing fast. If a week has gone by and your image ad unit hasn't acquired a Play button, it's probably not going to. So turn that image ad back into a text ad.

The second is to follow the strategy I·use at DealofDay.com. **I've placed two rectangular ads at the top of the page to make them unmissable but one of them is an image ad.**

Google no longer allows publishers to place related images right next to ad units to draw attention to them but you <u>can</u> put an image ad next to a text ad. If that image ad becomes a video ad, you're going to earn more money. If it stays an image ad, it's going to pull eyes into your ad zone.

This is about the only time I can think of when an image ad might be better than a text ad.

And when you do get video ads, there are also a couple of things that you can do to make the most of them...

Adding video to your Web pages for example, is a breeze. There are millions of clips available for free use on the Web, and there's nothing to stop you from shooting your own short.

If your site regularly receives a video ad from AdSense, placing one or two more videos on those pages would help the ad blend into the site and increase clicks.

Video ads are still fairly new on AdSense, but I'm really excited about them. I think we're going to be seeing a lot more of them in the future and they're going to really prove their worth.

I'm optimistic about video ads. I'm not sure yet about Gadget ads.

These are rich media ads that might contain animation, Flash games and interactive content. At the moment advertisers are big brands like Coca-Cola and I suspect it's likely to stay that way. Ads like these cost a lot more to design and program than a text ad, a graphic ad or even a home-made video ad.

They can pay by impression or by click but I'm skeptical that you'll get many clicks. An early test showed that only a third of one percent of viewers actually interacted with the ad.

The problem is that they just look too much like ads. Most users have learnt to ignore them.

If you do want to test them though, you'll need to opt in to receive image ads. Apparently the most popular sizes for gadgets are rectangles, leaderboards and skyscrapers.

Some ads might do well — such as those for movies or which have an attractive built-in game — but on the whole, I expect you'll find that a well-blended text ad unit will do better.

Fig. 3.11 This kind of Gadget ad could do well. But will others —and how much will it cost you to find out?

3. How To "Tweak" Your Ads To Make Them "Click"!

3.9 Link Units — Great Little Stocking Fillers

An ad format that has already proved its worth, when used correctly, is link units.

If you've ever bought Christmas presents for children, you've probably bought stocking fillers. You dole out hundreds of bucks on some state-of-the-art electronic gizmo, toss in a couple of toy cars that cost a dollar each just to fill up space and give the kid more to unwrap... then watch him spend 90 percent of his time playing with the car that cost 10 percent of your total gift budget.

Ad Link units have the potential to be equally profitable.

They're very small, almost unnoticeable... but when used well, they can be extremely effective.

Ad Link units let you place a box on your site that contains four or five links. They come in sizes ranging from 20 x 90 to 200 x 90, and are really meant to be placed on a sidebar.

Because you can place both Ad Link units as well as other ad units on the page, you might find that the choice helps: if a user doesn't spot something interesting in one type of ad block, he might spot it on another.

Where Ad Links differ from other types of ads is that they only display a list of topics that Google believes are relevant to the content of your pages. They don't display the ads themselves. When a visitor clicks on a topic, Google pops up a new window with targeted ads.

It can be argued that the Ad Links are ineffective because like video ads, people have to go through two clicks in order for you to get paid. That's right, once again, you're only getting paid for the *second* click (but that does mean you can check to see which ads your users are being served.)

But it can also be argued that if someone is taking the time to click on a topic, then they are probably very interested in the link, and are likely to click an actual advertisement on the resulting page. Some people have found that just about everyone who clicks on an Ad Link will click on the ads that appear on the next page.

I have tested Ad Links on multiple sites and have seen vast differences in results. That makes it more difficult to say whether or not they are for you.

In the first case, I placed the Ad Links on an information-based site with a very general audience. The results were nothing to write home about. Let's just say that you could just about buy a large candy bar with the results I saw.

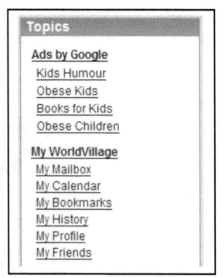

A cunningly disguised link unit at Worldvillage.com.

In the second case, I placed the Ad Links on a product specific site with a narrow audience. The results were fantastic! We're talking about figures that are greater than what someone might make flipping burgers in one day.

The conclusions should be obvious. If you're going to use an Ad Links unit campaign. You need to put them:

1.   **On a site with a specific field of interest.** A general site will give you general ads — and few clicks.

2.   **Above the fold with few other links.** For Ad Links, this is crucial: If your users are going to click a link, it should be a link that gives you money.

It's also a good idea to keep your Ad Link units for sites with high-paying keywords. If someone comes to your site seeking out information or a product on a top-notch keyword, they tend to be more likely to click as a result.

There are two kinds of link units: **vertical units** and **horizontal units**. Vertical link units are great slotted into sidebars. They just look like a natural extension of the link list.

But horizontal link units can be at least as effective. Since they were introduced, they really have become an extremely useful tool.

Some users have reported increases in CTR as high as 200 percent using these units!

Instead of piling the links one on top of the other—which is great for putting above lists of links but stand out too clearly when placed in text—the horizontal ads blend in perfectly when placed on pages with articles.

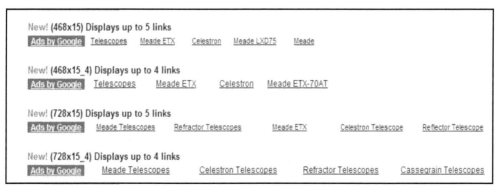

*Fig. 3.12 Horizontal Ad Link units are great for inserting into articles
and show very clearly which keywords your site is generating.*

You can use up to three Ad Link units per page so they're definitely worth slipping into a long article. You probably shouldn't put them at the bottom of a page where they'll be very easy to miss, but there are plenty of other places where these sorts of ads can work very, very well.

For example, a horizontal ad unit can be a great alternative to a leaderboard. It's much more subtle and takes up less space on the page — definitely something to experiment with to see which of the two brings you the highest revenues.

Or you could use them to separate forum or blog entries. As a horizontal unit, they can be very effective as frames that give people somewhere easy to go when they reach the end of a text unit.

One great use for horizontal link units though is on directory pages. If you have a Web page that contains tables of links, slipping a horizontal link unit above or below them — or both — can make the ads look like a part of the directory.

It almost makes you want to build a directory just to try it out!

Fig. 3.13 A horizontal link unit at the top of the page at BetaNews.com. Would a leaderboard have produced better revenues in that position? Again, something that can easily be tested.

3.10 Expanded Text Ads — Shrinking Control Or Expanded Income?

Take a look at the ad format samples on the AdSense site and you'll see a bunch of squares and rectangles filled with ads. Most of those ad units will contain more than one ad. On those units that do contain just the one ad, like the button or the half-banner, the ad will fill the space neatly and look pretty subtle.

You might be surprised then to put a skyscraper or a leaderboard on your site and find just one giant ad, written in super-sized text.

All the effort you've put into picking the right ad for your site, testing to see which formats work best and calculating which will give you the most clicks will have gone right out of the window.

You've prepared your site to serve multiple ads that look like content, and instead you're handing out a single ad that just screams "Don't click me!"

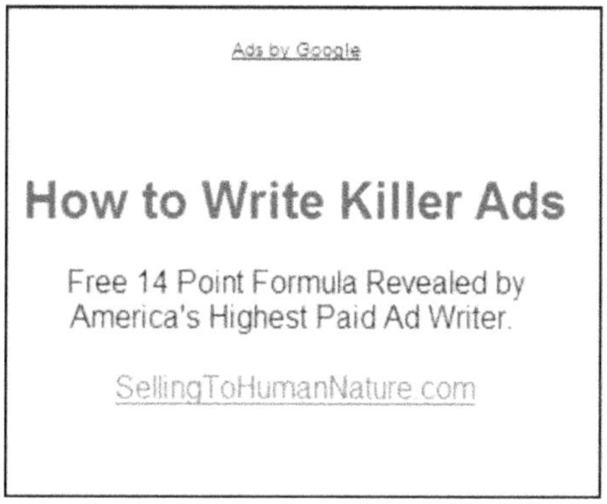

This can happen sometimes, but it's not a reason to panic. It might even be a reason to celebrate.

There are two possible reasons that Google is sending you these expanded text ads.

Fig. 3.14 You can't miss that! An expanded text ad strikes JoelComm.com.

The first possible reason is that you've been <u>keyword-targeted</u>. Google keeps track of your results (just like you should be doing) and tries to serve up the number of ads for your page that will bring in the highest amount of income. That might be four ads in a unit. Or just the one.

Frankly, I'm a touch skeptical that showing one ad is going to bring me more revenues than showing several. But I'm prepared to give AdSense the benefit of the doubt.

If I see that Google is giving me one ad, I'll compare the results for that one ad to the previous results that I've had serving multiple ads in the same unit. If I find that my revenues have dropped I can either block that ad using my filters or just ask AdSense not to give me any more single ads.

But if I find that the expanded text ad is giving me more money, I might still be worried. I know that users are more likely to click ads that look like content. I also know that they prefer to have a choice of ads rather than just one option.

If I'm getting more clicks then with just one ad, it could well be that I have been doing something wrong with that ad unit in the past. I would want to look at how well it's been optimized and whether it's in the right place to bring in the best income.

It could well be that this single ad is a high-payer and works better with little competition. But it could also be that getting that one ad is a warning that something was wrong with the way you've laid out that ad unit on your site.

You might want to try some different strategies to see if they'll increase your revenues when the multiple ads come back.

3. How To "Tweak" Your Ads To Make Them "Click"!

There is another possibility though. You might have been <u>placement-targeted</u>.

This is a whole different ball game. It means that an advertiser has spotted your site and asked Google to run their ads on it.

In the past, they could only do that on a CPM basis. You received a set fee for every thousand impressions.

Because you were no longer dealing with tempting people to click, you didn't care how much your ad looks like an ad. In fact you might even want it to look like an ad, if that's what will keep the advertiser happy.

That's no longer the case. Now advertisers can also place ads on cost-per-click basis. That means you should still blend your units into the page so that they don't look like ads.

The most important point to bear in mind here is that you want to make sure that you're not losing money. It might be very nice for the advertiser to have exclusive control over a particular spot on your page but if you can make more money serving CPC ads in that space, then you need to make sure that your site is working for you and not for the advertiser.

Again, watch your stats for a week and see if the revenues you receive for your impressions are higher than those you receive for your clicks.

Most publishers do find that placement targeted ads — even those that pay on a CPM basis — pay better, especially on sites with high traffic rates. After all, you're getting paid for every visitor who comes to your site rather than just those that click, so all you have to do to increase your revenue is increase your traffic. As long as each impression pays more than you're paying for the traffic, you're going to be making a profit. That should be easy to calculate.

If you find the revenues are lower though, then you'll want to boot that ad off and go back to serving conventional ads. You can do that by opting out of showing placement-targeted ads (you're automatically opted in) or even better, use the Review Center to block selected advertisers.

In general, the biggest problem with these sorts of campaigns is not lower revenues; it's that you've got no idea how long they're going to last which makes it difficult for you to take advantage of them. If you knew, for example, that you were going to get paid per impression for the next two weeks, then you'd want to buy in as much traffic as possible for that period, provided that you were paying less than you were earning.

And because you wouldn't care about CTR for those CPM campaigns, You could also lay off the optimization and focus on making your site more attractive to users.

But you can't tell when your site is going to be used for a CPM campaign and you can't tell how long it's going to last either. That means there's little point in making major changes to your optimization; you might have to rebuild it the next day.

The best strategy then when you spot a placement-targeted ad on your site is to keep a close eye on the cash flows. Buy in more traffic if you can do it profitably but for the most part, just enjoy the extra income!

3.11 Seasons Greeting With Themed Units

There is one more type of ad unit that you can use on your site. You just can't use it all the time. Every time a holiday rolls around, Google brings out new ad units with seasonal themes.

The designs themselves vary according to season and location (users in Europe, for example, won't see Thanksgiving ads).

In general, I always say that your ads should be unobtrusive but I like these themed ads. They're eye-catching without looking like banners. When it's holiday-time, it's always worth checking out the format page again and seeing what's available.

To sum up the different types of ad format then...

- **Leaderboards** are best at the top of the page;
- **Squares and rectangles** can be embedded into text itself;
- **Vertical ads and buttons** should slip down the side of the page;
- **Vertical link units** should be placed next to link lists;
- **Horizontal link units** can go at the top of the page, between blog entries or above and below directories;
- **Image ads** should rarely be used at all;
- **Themed ads** can be slotted in at holiday time;
- And **Video ads** should be used whenever possible.

Those are the general rules governing ad formats. They're worth knowing because they're a good place to start.

They're also worth knowing because you can't break the rules until you know what they are... and that's when the fun really begins!

4. USING COLORS TO INCREASE YOUR CLICKS

4.1 Design Your Website To Highlight Adsense

I once went to a fashion show where each model wore the exact same black outfit for the entire duration of the show. Boring? Hardly! The show was intended to showcase platinum jewelry, and the outfits were designed to enhance the jewelry — instead of distracting the audience.

You don't have to make all the pages on your website identical (or black). But you do want to make sure that the look of your page draws attention to the ads — and makes them appear as attractive and as valuable as platinum jewelry.

Many websites have strong graphic elements that catch the eye — usually at the expense of the AdSense units.

> If you're using AdSense, be judicious in the selection of fonts, font size, colors, images, tables and other visual aspects of your website.
>
> **Draw subtle attention to your AdSense units. Make them the stars of your show!**

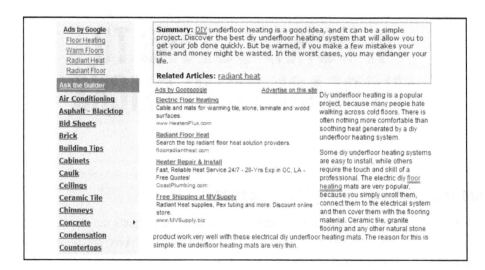

Fig. 4.1 On this website, Tim Carter employs subtle design and placement to make AdSense the center of attraction. Check out his work at www.askthebuilder.com.

4.2 Make The Border Go!

You can more than DOUBLE your clickthroughs with this one simple tweak!

Even before the Internet, ads in newspapers and magazines were marked off with a thick, heavy border. No wonder borders and boxes have come to symbolize advertising messages.

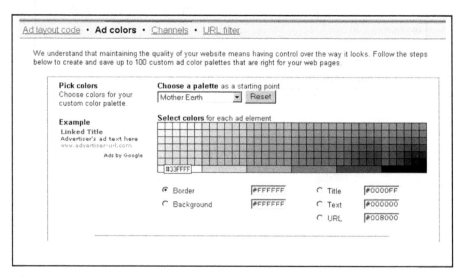

*Fig. 4.2 It's always easier to work with a white background. If your page background is white, you can instantly see the results with the **Example** ad next to the color palette.*

Ads with prominent borders make your pages look cluttered. They distract the eye from the ad text, while marking off the ad blocks from the rest of the content.

> Google provides an extensive color palette in your administrative area. Use it to tweak the look of your ads to suit your Web page.

With just one simple click, you can match the color of <u>your ad's border</u> with the background color of <u>your Web page</u>. When the border blends with the background, it frees up loads of space. The page looks instantly neater and the ads look more inviting.

Make sure you also pick a matching <u>background color for the ad</u>. The ad's background must match the page background on which the ad will appear.

If the ad appears in a table, match the table background color with the ad background color.

The key is to blend the background and border color with the page, so that the text looks like an integral part of your web content.

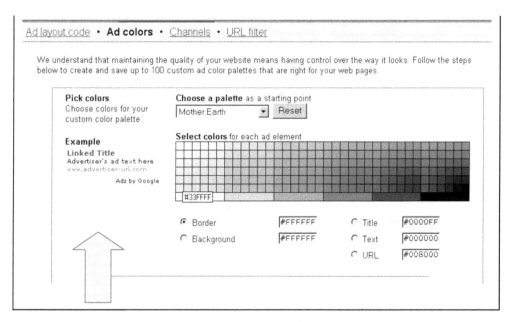

Fig. 4.3 Don't forget to match the <u>background color for your ad</u> with the background color of <u>your web page</u>. Even with a matching border, the ad in the **Example** *above sticks out against the white background.*

4.3 Text Is Design Too!

That's right: the text size, font and color must match the other text elements. If the text color of the ads is the same as the text in the body of your page, it'll help the ads blend into the site and make the reader feel that you've endorsed them.

And if the size of the font in the ads is the same as the size of the main body of the content, it will have the same effect: they'll look like part of your site and not something brought in by Google.

That's the sort of blending that translates into clicks.

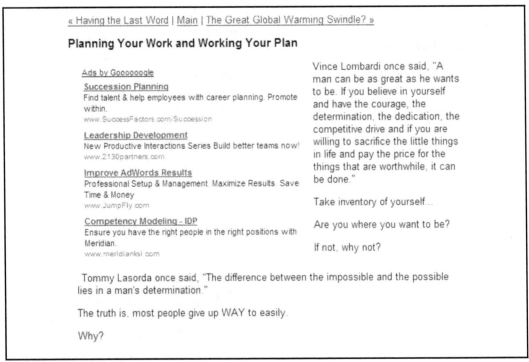

Fig 4.4 **Format your text ads to maximize clicks!** *On my blog,*
I have removed the border and matched the ad's background color
and fonts to my content. See more at www.joelcomm.com.

This **3-way matching** (titles, text and background) can generate excellent clickthrough rates.

Too many text styles add clutter and can confuse your visitors. Instead, try every legitimate way to make the ads look like a part of your web content.

Using the colors to make sure that **your ads don't look like ads** is straightforward enough. Google has always provided plenty of color options so that you could easily match the ads to the content and blend them into your site.

Optimizing your text though was always a lot harder.

Google only provided ads in one font and that font only came in one size.

That meant publishers had to work backwards. If they didn't want the ads to stand out like a bunch of lost penguins in the Sahara, they had to make sure that they didn't use fonts on their Web page that were outrageously creative or in strange sizes.

In general, that made sense anyway. Because different browsers display fonts and sizes slightly differently, conservative choices were always the best way to make sure that what you were seeing on your screen was what everyone was seeing on their screen too.

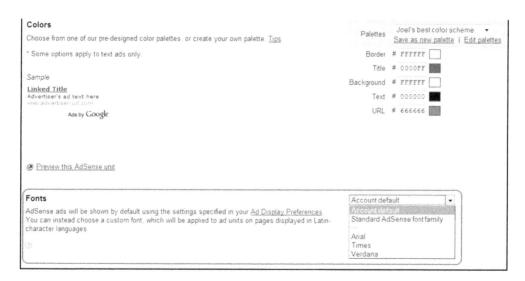

Fig 4.5 Choosing a font for one ad unit. No 57 varieties here...

Now though, Google is allowing publishers to be a little more adventurous.

The company has added an option that lets us change the ad font... to one of four choices.

We can choose between Arial, Verdana, Times New Roman or "Standard AdSense Font Family" which is usually either Arial or Verdana.

So no Georgia. No MS Trebuchet. And no range of sizes.

Which one should you choose?

Right... the one you've chosen for your website. And if you haven't chosen one of those fonts for your website, then you might want to try one with a matching ad unit and see if it improves your results.

Harder than choosing the right font for the ads though will be applying them to the ads.

If all your Web pages use the same font, then the best option is to visit your My Account page then click "edit" in the "Ad Display Preference" section. Choose the font you want and it will be applied across all of your ad units automatically.

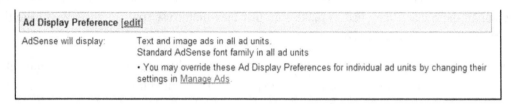

Fig 4.6 Hit "edit" and you'll be able to change all your ad units at once. Neat.

If you use different fonts on different pages — or if you want to test different ad fonts on different pages — then you'll need to apply the fonts to the ad units individually. To do that, you'll need visit the Manage Ads page in your account, choose the unit you want to change and pick the font from the drop-down menu.

Any units whose fonts you change manually will be excluded if you then apply a different font to all of your units automatically.

4.4 Blue Is Best

So you want to get rid of the border. You want to get your ads the same color as the text on the rest of your page and the background matching the background color of your Web page. And you want the font of the ad to match the font on the page.

But what about the link itself, the line the user is actually going to click? What color should that be?

That's an easy one: blue.

I used to say that *all* the text in the ad should match the text on your page, including the link. After seeing an article about the benefits of keeping the links blue — and testing extensively — I don't say that any more.

The logic is that users have come to expect links on websites to be blue. Just as they expect stop signs to be red and warning signs to be yellow, so they expect their links to blue.

That means people are more likely to click on a blue link than a link in any other color.

The line in your AdSense code that sets the color of your link is the one that says:

Google_color_link = "#color";

"#color" is the hexadecimal number for the color you want to use. You should make sure that number is #0000FF.

Keep your link blue and you can experience an increase in clickthroughs as high as 25 percent!

4.5 Where Did My URL Go?

You can change the color of your text and you can make sure that your links scream, "I'm a FREE road to where you want to go!"

But you still have to display the URL, even though it means that people could type it into their browser later, cutting you out of a commission. It's one of Google's rules. You just don't have to display the URL in a way that people can see it.

One legitimate trick is to change the URL display color to match the text description color. Now the eye will be drawn to the hyperlink instead of the URL. Google provides these tools for you. Why not use them?

Note that the 728 x 90 leaderboard and the 468 x 60 banner do not display the URL line by Google's design. It is not a mistake and you will not get in trouble for the URL not appearing with these ad blocks. That's just the way they've done it.

4.6 Deliberate Mismatching

When it comes to choosing colors, I recommend 3-way matching and using blue for the links. But there is another strategy that you can use.

You can deliberately mismatch your ad colors and styles, *provided you keep it to the top of your page*.

This distinction generates two powerful 'zones' and therefore two types of experience for the visitor.

The first zone is always at the top of the first page. The titles and text colors match colors found in the banner graphic heading. (Important — the URL links are hidden, so only certain text ads will allow you to do this.)

The end result is that these ads, placed above the banner graphic look like key control points for your site and are just more likely to be clicked. The visitor feels that they are visiting another major area of that site.

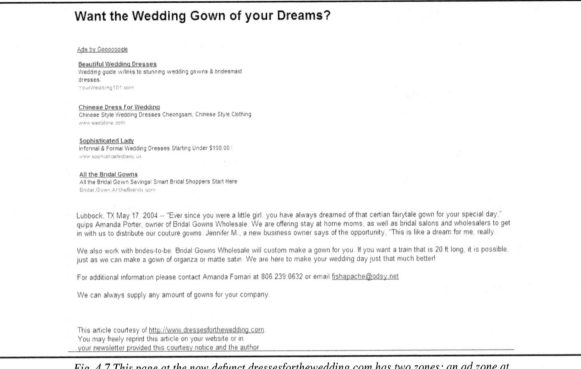

Fig. 4.7 This page at the now defunct dressesforthewedding.com has two zones: an ad zone at the top and a free article beneath. Implementing this design increased revenues FIVE-FOLD!

4.7 Changing The Look Of Your Ads

The strategies I've provided in this chapter will all help to improve your clickthrough rates. That's what happened when I used them and it's what happened when other people used them.

But one of the most important strategies you can use with AdSense is to experiment.

If you find that a slightly larger ad format gives you better results, for example, then obviously, you should use the bigger one.

In the past, changing your ads meant copying the code and pasting it into your site again.

Today, things are a bit easier than that.

When you create your ad code, you'll be asked to give that code a name. *Make sure that name tells you exactly where the ad will be placed and its format.*

Whenever you want to change the way an ad looks, you'll be able to pull up that code on your AdSense center and make the changes. Your ad will be updated automatically within the next ten minutes… unless you want to change the size of your ads. That you'll still have to do manually by pasting in the new code.

5. HOW TO MAXIMIZE VISIBILITY AND RESPONSE

5.1 Ad Placement: Where To Put Your Ads?

Location is everything. The world's best ad won't deliver if it isn't visible in the first place. But after much experimentation with Google AdSense, I know that the most visible ads aren't always the most effective. In fact, they're likely to get ignored as 'blatant advertising'.

What does work is *wise* placement. Put them where your content is most likely to interest and engage your visitors.

> You can create several 'points of interest' with the wise use of graphics, tables and other layout techniques.

Once you have your visitors' attention with engaging and meaningful content, they are most likely to read and click on relevant ads. And that is precisely what Google wants — "educated" clicks from real prospects, not random visits from bored people.

Here are a few simple tips to make your ads 'click'!

5.2 Go With The 'Flow'

Identify the reading patterns of your visitors. What draws their attention first? What makes them click?

Like I said, you want to put your ads in areas that draw your visitors in with interesting content. There's no point in putting your ads in some out of the way place where no one ever looks. Your users will follow your content, so you need to make sure that your ads follow that content too.

Look at the design and layout of your Web page, identify the places that you think most of your users look — and mark each of them as a likely spot to put your ads.

Google actually offers a pretty neat tool to help you identify where your users are most likely to look. Their heat map at https://www.google.com/support/adsense/bin/static.py?page=tips.html sums up the options pretty well:

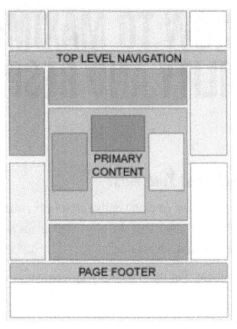

Fig. 5.1 Google's Heat Map shows an "average" site's hot spots. The darker areas are the regions where people look most frequently. But remember, no site is average. Where do your visitors look most?

Google says that certain areas are more effective than others. Researchers have also found that when people look at a website, their eyes start in the top left hand corner and then travel down the page from left to right.

All of this is true but the hottest areas can vary from site to site. You will need to experiment to find the very best places for you.

5.3 Above The Fold

One general rule on the Internet is that people spend most of their time on a site "above the fold."

The first thing people do when they reach a website is to absorb as much information as possible before they start scrolling. The part of the page that they can see without scrolling is called "above the fold."

That's where you want your ads.

The number of links that appear above the fold affect how likely people are to click on your AdSense ads. *That's why more ads doesn't always mean more money!*

Google always puts the top-paying ads on the top and the lowest-paying ones at the bottom.

If you have a stack with three or more ads, the cheaper ads might steal attention away from high-paying ads and clutter up your website.

You don't want ads and links competing against each other. If you want to increase your earnings per click, remember: Less is More! And that's particularly true above the fold.

Let's take a look at two sample pages:

Fig. 5.2 This page that used to run on www.MegaBookshop.com had a search form, a featured product, category links and AdSense ads, all above the fold.

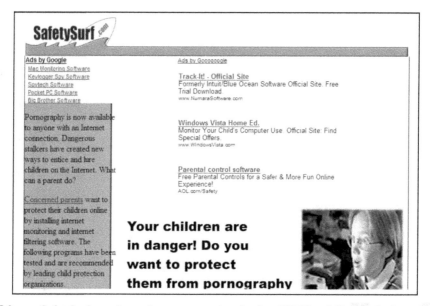

Fig. 5.3 www.SafetySurf.com is not the most attractive site, but ONLY has AdSense ads above the fold.

Now, which of these sites' ads do you think brings a higher clickthrough rate? You guessed it. The second site has *triple* the clickthrough rate of the first site. The moral of the story? If you want to maximize your AdSense clicks, give your visitors fewer choices above the fold!

5.4 Using Tables

I've already mentioned that one of the principles of a high clickthrough rate is to make your sites blend into the page. The more you position your sites to blend into the page, the better your clickthrough rate will be.

One very neat way to help your ads blend into the site is to place them in tables.

In the example below, Chris Pirillo again skillfully dropped his AdSense into a <table> for a clean and attractive look that turns AdSense into a new focal point.

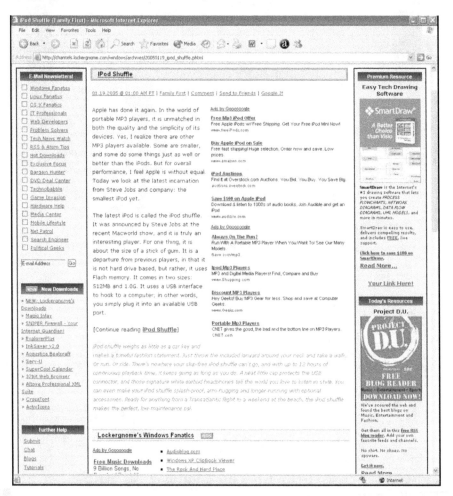

Fig 5.4 Note how clean the tables make the ads look.

Want to get the same results with your web page? Dave Taylor at www.intuitive.com shares this simple code to create a left-aligned table containing AdSense. Just paste this code where you want AdSense to appear. **Easy!**

Left-aligned table with AdSense:

<table border="0" align="left"><tr><td>

Google adsense code goes here

</td></tr></table>

Right-aligned table with AdSense:

<table border="0" align="right"><tr><td>

Google adsense code goes here

</td></tr></table>

5.5 Complementing Your Ads

Everything I've discussed so far has been about placing your ads where your users will be looking. That's pretty easy. But there's an alternative strategy, which can be very powerful: bringing your users to your ads.

You have to be careful here though. Google forbids you from saying to users "Look over here and click on the ads... I want the money." And that's reasonable. But with some clever design work, you can still guide your users to look in that direction.

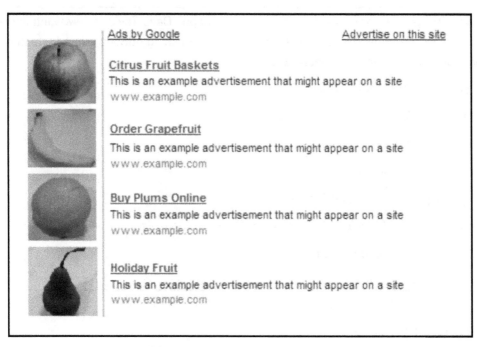

Fig. 5.5 Google says: "Don't try this at home..."

The rule to remember here is that **elements attract eyes**. When a user loads a Web page, he's always going to look at various things on the page, not just the text. That's especially true of images, which is why one popular strategy was to place pictures related to the content of the ad right next to the ad unit.

Google has changed its terms to forbid that practice specifically.

Not surprisingly, when Google brought out that rule, it created a mild panic among publishers who rushed to change their page layouts. It didn't help that Google didn't specify how far images should be from the ad units. The company just says that the images and the ads should not be lined up "in a way that suggests a relationship" between them.

That's vague enough to give Google plenty of latitude to ban publishers who think they're doing nothing wrong.

Fortunately, I haven't heard of anyone being banned for failing to move their ads, and I suspect that you'd get a warning letter before any action was taken.

So if you can't put related images next to ads to draw attention to them, what can you do?

I've already talked about placing a text ad unit next to an image ad unit. That's one strategy you could use.

You could also place an *unrelated* image next to an ad unit. Again, as long as there's no suggestion of a relationship between the image and the ad unit, you'll be safe.

For example, at SafetySurf.com. I put a link unit at the top of the page. It's above the side bar, which is where many people put link units, but it's also directly beneath the icon.

People are always going to look at the icon. When they look at the icon, they'll see the ads.

Fig. 5.6 One way to place an image next to an ad SafetySurf.com.

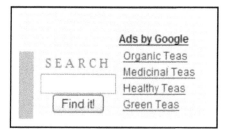

Fig. 5.7 A new use for a search box at FamilyFirst.com.

There are all sorts of ways you can do this, but probably the best method is to first place your ads and then think about which images you can place near them.

Of course, you don't just have to use images. You could also use a "Submit" button, a "next" link or anything else that users will have to look at on your page.

A search box for example is an excellent spot. You know your users are about to look for something and click away. Why not offer them some of your own options.

There's a good chance that pulling your users' eyes in this way will increase your click-through rates.

6. CONTROLLING YOUR ADS

6.1 Attracting Relevant Ads

Getting the color and placement right will help improve your clickthrough rate. But neither of those will affect which ads your site serves.

In theory, Google controls the ads that appear on your site. You don't get to choose them at all. In practice, there are a few things that you can do to stop irrelevant ads from appearing and ensure that you get the ads that give you cash.

The more relevant the ads, the greater the chance that a user will click and you'll earn money.

The most important factor is obviously going to be your content. Google's crawlers will check your site and serve up ads based on the keywords and the content on your page.

Bear in mind that Google's crawlers can't read graphics or Flash or pretty much anything that isn't text. I'll talk about content in detail in chapter 11 but for now, remember that if you want to keep your ads relevant, you've got to have the sort of page that Google can understand and use to give you the ads you want.

6.2 Keep The Title, Directory And Headlines Relevant

How exactly the crawlers read pages is a secret guarded about as closely as Coca Cola's special syrup formula. One thing that does seem to have an effect though is the title of your URLs and files.

When you create your pages and view them on your computer before uploading them to the server, you should find that AdSense serves up ads related to the name of the directory that holds the page. That gives a pretty big clue as to at least one of the things that Google is looking at: the name of the directory.

Actually, it's not just the name of the directory that's important. The name of the file plays a big part too.

If you have a website about wedding trains and the title of one of your pages is trains.php for example, there's a good chance that you'll get ads about Amtrak and Caltrain. That wouldn't give you many clicks. Change the name of the file to weddingtrains.php and there's a much better chance that you'll see ads related to weddings.

If you find that the ads that are appearing on your site have nothing to do with your content, the first places to look are your directory and your title. Make them more relevant to your content and you should find that you get better ads.

Another place to look is your headlines. Instead of using a <font> tag for your heading, try using the <h1> tag with headings that contain your keywords. That should help them to stand out to the crawlers.

And if you don't have any headlines at all, try adding some.

6.3 Finding Keywords

We know that Google's crawlers search websites for keywords, then reports back and tells the company what kind of ads to send to the site. If your site is about pension plans for example, then your keywords would be things like "retirement", "401k" and "pension".

Getting the right keywords on your site won't just make your ads relevant; it will also help you to make sure that the ads you get are the ones that pay the most.

There are all sorts of tools available on the Web that tell you how much people are prepared to pay for keywords. www.overture.com and www.googlest.com let you see how much people are prepared to pay, and WordTracker provides a wealth of keyword research tools that unearth pure gold. You can check it out at www. WordTracker.com.

Again, you don't want to build a site just to cash in on a high paying keyword but if you know that "401k" pays more than "retirement" for example, then it makes sense to use the higher paying keywords more than the lower paying ones.

See chapter 14 for more on finding the most up-to-date high paying keywords.

6.4 Keyword Density

You'll need the right keywords to get the right ads. But you'll also need the right amount of keywords.

There's no golden rule for putting the right number of keywords on a page to get the ads you want. You'll just have to experiment. It also seems to be the case that keyword density is counted across pages, especially for high-paying keywords. If you have a site that's generally about cars and you write a page for car rental, a higher-paying keyword, you might find that you need to produce several pages about car rental before you get the ads.

In general though, if you find that your ads are missing the point of your page and that your titles are all correct, then the next step would be to try mentioning your keywords more often and make sure that they're all finely focused. For example, talking about "fire extinguishers" is likely to get you better results than talking generally about "safety equipment."

6.5 Keyword Placement

It shouldn't really matter where you put your keywords, should it? As long as the right words are on the right page in the right amount, that should be enough to get you relevant ads, right?

Wrong.

One of the strangest results that people have had using AdSense is that putting keywords in particular places on the page can have an effect on the ads the site gets.

The most important place on your webpage is directly beneath the AdSense unit. The keywords you place there could influence your ads.

For example, mentioning clowns in the space directly beneath the AdSense box could give you ads about circuses and red noses!

Keeping that in mind, you could play with your ads in all sorts of ways. If you had a site about camping for example, you might find that you're getting lots of ads about tents and sleeping bags, which would be fine. But if you also wanted to make sure that one or two of your ads were about Yosemite or mobile homes, then mentioning those keywords once or twice on the page directly below the AdSense units could give you ads for sites with that sort of content too.

Bear in mind though that you'll often find that you get ads that try to combine the main thrust of your site with the words in that keyword space below the ad box. So if you had a site about gardening and you mentioned "cabbages" beneath the ad box, you're more likely to get ads about growing cabbages than ads about cabbage recipes.

Experimenting with the placement of the keywords could allow you to control at least one or two of the ads you receive and help keep them varied. That's definitely something to try.

6.6 Keyword Frames

One of the reasons that websites don't always receive relevant ads may be that all the navigation and other non-content words affect the way Google reads the page. If your links and other words take up lots of space, it could well skew your results.

One way to avoid your navigation affecting your ads is simply to create frames. You put all of your content in your main frame and the navigation material in a separate frame. Only the "content frame" has the Google code (google_page_url = document.location), so your keywords won't be diluted by non-relevant words.

6.7 Section Targeting

Probably the most effective way to ensure the crawlers read the keywords you want to emphasize though is to use Section Targeting. This is a fantastic technique. By simply inserting a couple of lines of HTML code into your Web page, you can tell the crawler which parts of your site are the most important and ensure that you get ads relevant to that content.

The lines you want to use to emphasize particular sections of your Web page are:

<!-- google_ad_section_start -->

Section text.

<!-- google_ad_section_end -->

The rest of the page won't be ignored, but those particular lines will receive a heavier weighting. If you want to tell the crawlers to ignore particular sections, you can use these lines:

<!-- google_ad_section_start(weight=ignore) -->

Section text.

<!-- google_ad_section_end -->

You can highlight (and de-emphasize) as many or as few sections as you wish, but what you can't do is use these instructions solely to highlight keywords. So you can't put them around particular single words or phrases on your page and hope to see ads that relate only to those terms.

In fact, Google recommends that you highlight a sizeable portion of text — as much as 20 percent — for the targeting to be most effective. The result of targeting small amounts of text could be irrelevant ads, public service ads... or even a banning if you deliberately tried to bring up ads that have nothing to do with your site.

Section Targeting is probably most useful if you have a Web page that covers lots of different topics. So if you had a blog about MP3 players but had written an article about rap music for example, you could use Section Targeting to ensure that you didn't lose ads about the music players to ads about rap music. Or you could tell the crawlers to ignore your readers' comments and focus on your own entries.

And presumably, there's nothing wrong with stuffing a paragraph with keywords related to your subject and telling the crawlers to focus on that section to ensure that your ads stay targeted.

It's definitely something that you want to play with.

If there's one problem with Section Targeting though, it's that it can take up to two weeks before you see the results — the time it can take for the crawler to re-visit your page. So it's not a fast process and that can make it a bit of a blunt tool. But it's not blunt enough to be ignored.

6.8 No 'Baiting'!

Often I've clicked through a 'promising' website, only to find reams of keyword spam, interspersed with AdSense. Websites like these make AdSense look bad.

Keyword spam may trick search spiders, but your human visitors will leave disappointed.

People hate being 'baited' by a web site. Offer content that makes their visit worthwhile. **Address the needs and concerns of your visitors with original content.**

Quality content builds trust and loyalty — and that, in turn, makes people want to click. Search rankings may change, but loyal visitors keep coming back for more!

6.9 Changing Metatags

Metatags certainly aren't what they used to be, and in AdSense they're barely anything at all. There's a good chance that when it comes to deciding ad relevance, your metatags have no effect whatsoever.

I've already mentioned that the title of your page will have an effect. It's also very likely that the description does too.

But that doesn't mean that your metatags are completely irrelevant when it comes to AdSense. They aren't. They're only seem to be irrelevant when it comes to serving ads; they still play a role in search engine optimization and getting your site indexed faster.

6.10 Inviting The Robot

So far in this chapter, I've explained some of the ways that you can tweak your page to keep your ads relevant. But the changes you make won't have any effect until Google's robot stops by and re-indexes your page. What will generally happen is that once you upload your new page, you'll still get the old ads and you might have to wait some time before the robot visits it again and you can find out whether your changes have the right result.

To get the robot to stop by earlier, reload the page in your browser, and then again a few minutes later. Do not click on any of the ads just reload and wait a few minutes before attempts.

This doesn't always work but with a bit of luck, you should find that you receive new ads within a few minutes.

6.11 Google Ads Preview

Don't want to wait for the robot? No problem. The Google Ads Preview tool at http://googleadspreview. blogspot.com lets you see the ads your site is likely to receive right away.

Google has its own tool for this, but this program by Digital Inspiration is much better. It lets you compare different programs and formats side by side.

When you're just starting out, that's not really important. But when you're combining AdSense with a Chitika unit it's useful to see what effect a single change can have across the different ads you're displaying.

You can also compare the AdSense ads with those served by Yahoo! Publishers Network.

And here's the real kicker: **the Google Ads Preview Tool also lets you toss in keywords and see which ads turn up.**

Try it! Surf over to the site, toss in a keyword relevant to your site and see what ads you're likely to receive.

Note that I said which ads you're likely to receive, not which ads you *will* receive.

That's an important difference. Google uses all sorts of criteria to decide which ads you're going to pick up. I'm not sure which criteria this preview tool uses to choose ads for keywords but I can't see it emulating Google completely.

Use the tool to preview the ads on your site and you're on pretty firm ground. You'll get a great impression of the ads you're likely to find on your site and you can either match your content to it or change your content to bring up some different ads. Use it to preview the ads you're likely to get with a certain keyword and you've got a guide to where those keywords can take you.

Either way, you've got a very useful tool.

6.12 Public Service Ads

The penalty for not getting your keyword placement and density right isn't just irrelevant ads. It could also be no ads at all. If Google can't find any relevant ads to give you, it could use your space to present public service ads, which are very nice but they don't pay you a penny. You might prefer to earn money and give it to a charity of your choice rather than give space on your site to a cause that Google chooses.

Google lets you get rid of that space by collapsing the ad, tossing in an image or by creating a color block in the same tone as the background color. But that seems like a waste to me. That space can earn you money. If something goes wrong with your contextualization, you want a back-up that brings revenue.

The most obvious solution is to specify an alternate URL in the event that Google has no ads for you. You can do this from your AdSense account. Instead of linking to the Red Cross or whoever it may be, you'll receive a link to a site that you've pre-chosen.

I've created my own default set of ads for various block sizes. You can see an example of this at www. worldvillage.com/336x280-1.html.

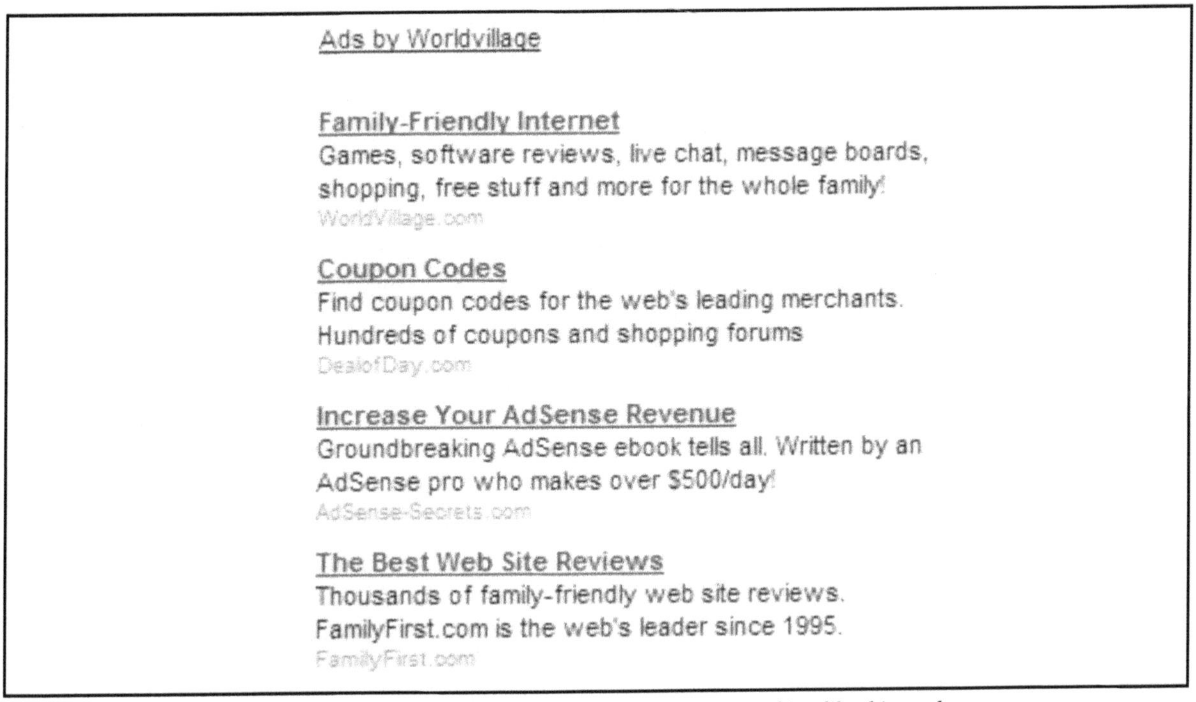

Fig. 6.1 My own version of AdSense. Just don't run something like this on the same page as real AdSense ads or Google will be unhappy with you.

A great replacement for pesky PSAs, right?

Just remember that Google doesn't like it when publishers use ad units that mimic AdSense ads ON THE SAME PAGE as live AdSense ads. That's why I only use this format for PSA replacements.

But there are plenty of other options.

For example, you could use this space to deliver image-based ads that come from your server. For offers that pay per action (clicks or signups), I like to use WebSponsors.com. You can sign up for a free account and find new ways to monetize your unused ad space.

Probably the best way to turn that wasted space into revenue though is to place a Chitika ad there. I talk about Chitika later in this book, in the chapter about other ad systems. The company has some fantastic looking ad units, and they can be used in conjunction with AdSense.

Having a Chitika ad automatically replace a PSA ad is, I feel, the perfect solution until you manage to sort out the problem with your AdSense unit.

The principle is the same as the AdSense-like ad units I used to use: create a blank page on your site, add your Chitika code and use the URL as your alternate AdSense URL.

It's really very simple and very effective.

6.13 Blocking Ads

Another useful way to control the ads you see on your site is to block ads you don't want using the Competitive Ad Filter. You can find it under the AdSense Setup Tab in your AdSense account. You can make the filter as narrow as a specific page and as wide as a complete domain.

Google only gives you a limit of 200 URLs to block, which isn't much. You might well find yourself burning through them pretty fast, especially if you try to block lower paying ads in favor of the higher-paying ones.

Playing with keywords, content and placement will give you much better results.

6.14 Placement Targeting

Most of the ads that appear on your site will have been placed there as a result of Google's contextualization program. AdSense figures out what your site's about and serves relevant ads. That's how the system works.

Some of the ads though might appear as a result of Placement Targeting.

Instead of crossing their fingers and hoping that their ads appear on good sites, advertisers are able to choose the sites on which they place their ads. They can even choose the *channels* on which to place their ads. I'll discuss how that can happen — and how you can encourage it to happen — when I describe channels in more detail in chapter 14.

Ads targeted in this way still have to compete with those submitted by other advertisers so they should improve the value of your clicks. But there is a risk...

While targeting keywords means that there's a chance that a competitor's ads will appear on your site, Placement Targeting lets competitors deliberately target rivals' sites.

To block these ads, you'll need to sign up for the **Ad Review Center**. (You'll find the link on the Competitive Ad Filter page under the AdSense Setup tab.)

One option here is initially set to "Run ads immediately" but you can also choose to hold the ads for 24 hours so that you can approve them. That's useful if you're worried about competitors targeting your site or want to stop some political ads from running on your pages. But ads put on hold aren't taking part in the auction for your spots so it could bring your click price down overall.

If you're confident that your site won't be targeted by competitors trying to take your traffic or you don't care about political ads, then let everything through. You'll earn more.

In the past, there was another way that publishers could target websites, and that was on the sites themselves. Publishers could place an "Advertise on this site" link next to their ads and lead advertisers to a landing page that they could stuff with information about their users. Google no longer offers this option but it doesn't mean that you shouldn't do it anyway.

You'll be able to cut out the middleman and take all of the ad revenue for yourself.

Place the link at the bottom of the page, so that it's not in the way and invite advertisers to submit their own ads. The link would just need to say something like "Advertise on this site." You'll then need a landing page with text that offers information about your users so that advertisers will know what they're getting. Something like this will do. You can take it and adapt it for your own site.

Thank you for advertising on FamilyFirst.com, the web's leading site for family-friendly web site reviews. Our users are typically traditional families, stay-at-home moms and parents of children aged between 3 and 16.

We've found that users respond most favorably to articles and links about filter software, children's DVDs and computer games, toys and family entertainment.

Highlighting these aspects of your business in your ad is likely to earn the highest number of clicks and the best conversions.

We look forward to helping your business grow! If you would like more information about advertising on FamilyFirst.com, including a quote for your campaign, please write to sales@FamilyFirst.com.

Most importantly though, you'll need to know how much you're currently receiving on average per click or per thousand impressions.

Google would only accept the top bids. You'll need to know what those are if you're not going to replace a high-paying ad with a low-paying one.

6.15 Does Location Matter For CPM Ads?

In a word, yes! This is what Google has to say about CPM ads, the type of ads you might well receive from a placement-targeted campaign (my emphasis):

> You'll earn revenue each time a CPM (cost per 1000 impressions, also known as *pay-per-impression*) ad is displayed on your site. You won't earn additional revenue for clicks on these ads.
>
> **Please note that the placement of CPM ads on your pages can affect the amount an advertiser pays for that impression.** Placing your CPM ad units *below the fold*, or in an otherwise *low-impact location*, may result in *lower earnings than if the ad unit was placed in a conspicuous location*.

So if you were thinking, "Great! I'll encourage clickthroughs above the fold *and* get paid per impression with an expanded text ad at the bottom of the page..." think again.

Google claims that CPM campaigns have to bid for space on publishers' websites in the same marketplace as CPC ads, and that therefore you would only receive a CPM ad if it's the highest paying option. If advertisers are paying less for a CPM ad at the bottom of a page, it's less likely then that you're going to get one down there.

Now, how Google is figuring out where on the page you're putting your ads beats me. Their love of Smart Pricing (see chapter 15) though, suggests that they could be comparing advertisers' sales results with the number of impressions and assuming that sites with high impressions and low sales have put the ads in out-of-the-way places.

Whichever method they're using, the end result is that you're still going to see higher revenues from ads in the best locations and less from the worst spots.

7. QUICKSTART ADSENSE: A STEP-BY-STEP GUIDE

You can be up and running with AdSense in just minutes. Sure, you'll need a bit more time if you want to use all of the advanced strategies and techniques I discuss in the rest of this book, but you don't have to wait until you've figured everything out before you can start earning with AdSense.

Remember, every minute that your site isn't showing online or isn't showing ads, you're tossing money down the drain.

If you don't have a site yet, or if you're not showing ads on your site, before you move on to the rest of this book, follow one of these guides. You'll be amazed at how easy it is to start making money with ads!

7.1 AdSense QuickStart Guide #1: Building A Blog

Blogging is probably the easiest way to get online with AdSense fast. The sites are already online, you don't have to worry about graphics and the domains are all set up.

All you have to do is sign up, write and earn!

Step 1: Surf to www.blogger.com

Complete the registration page, choose a name for your blog and pick a template.

Step 2: Apply For AdSense Through Blogger

Another form, another five minutes. It will take a day or two before your application is approved. In the meantime, you can play with Blogger's AdSense preview tool, and...

Step 3: Write Your First Blog Entry

Not sure what to write? Start with your family, spout off about a story in the news, put up pictures for your friends to see... it doesn't matter. Everyone has something that occupies their mind, that interests them or that they're good at. Put up anything. You can change it later but for now just get in the habit of writing to the Web. Once you've done it once you'll see how easy it can be — and how addictive.

Step 4: Play With Your Ads

Once AdSense has approved your application, you'll be able to start playing with your ads. You can change the colors, fix the font size, remove the border and move them into the sidebar if you wish. You can get everything geared up and ready to...

Step 5: Bring In The Traffic

It's taken you minutes to get your site set up. Now you have to let people know you're online. Chapter 21 will tell you how to bring in large amounts of traffic but for now you can start by telling your friends, swapping links with your favorite sites and submitting your site to the search engines. Hold off on the paid advertising though until you've got enough content to make it worthwhile. You're rolling!

7.2 AdSense QuickStart Guide #2:
Building An Ad-Supported Commercial Site With Zlio

Writing content is just one way to fill a site that will earn from advertising. Another is to display products for sale. That might sound hard but with a website, it's very, very easy.

You don't have to see the products, store the products, touch the products or mail the products. All you have to do is market the products... and take a cut of the sales price.

Usually, ads on commercial sites don't work too well. You want people to buy from you, not from a competitor. When you use Zlio.com— an online store-building service — to build your site though, you don't need to care who gives you the money... as long as someone does.

Step 1. Sign Up And Choose Your Store Name

Zlio's registration page is very simple. The only thing you'll need to consider is the name of the store. You might want to think about that for... maybe a minute. Just choose something that's simple to remember and which sums up the products you plan to sell.

Step 2. Pick A Template

There's no programming with Zlio. Pick one of eleven ready-built templates and you're ready to go.

Step 3. Add Products

Zlio has over three million different products that you can add to your store and receive commissions on sales or even payment for clicks. I'm sure you can find something you want to sell...

Step 4. Add AdSense

In addition to placing units containing products for sale, you can also include AdSense units. And Zlio's AdSense API makes it a breeze. You don't even have to go back to the AdSense site to get the code. It's all automated from Zlio's own site.

Step 5. Start Marketing

Building the site is easy. It will take about five minutes. Bringing in customers will be a bigger challenge and take a little longer. But it's nothing that can't be overcome with some hard work and steady learning.

7.3 AdSense QuickStart Guide #3: Building A Site From Scratch

Using an automated system like Blogger or Zlio is the easiest way to get started with AdSense but it's not for everyone. Create a complete website from scratch is going to take a little longer... but not a lot longer.

Step 1: Pick Up A Name

The first thing you'll need is a domain. You grab one of those at either GoDaddy.com or NetworkSolutions.com.

Step 2: Build Your Site

You can build your site yourself or hire someone to do it for you. Or you can take a pre-built template and pack it with your own content. Yahoo! has a program called SiteBuilder (http://webhosting.yahoo.com/ps/sb/index.php) that's packed with a good range of templates that you can use and play with but you'll have to upload the finished site onto Yahoo's servers. If you're in a rush, it's a great way to get online and earning fast.

Step 3: Create Your Content

Keep it simple! You don't have to pack your site with Flash images or anything fancy. Write about what you like! If you're into fun at the beach, create pages with reviews of your local sand spots. Into skiing? Discuss your favorite ski equipment. Everyone's got something that lights their fire. Decide what makes you burn and put it on your first site. You'll find that a site that interests you interests all the people like you... and gets you the sort of following that wins clicks.

Step 4: Apply For AdSense

Once your first pages are up and built (and none of this should take you more than a few hours) you're ready to apply to AdSense. Fill in the form and wait for the approval.

Step 5: Bring In The Traffic

While you're waiting for the first ads, you can start submitting your site to the search engines and building up the traffic.

Step 6: Play With Your Ads

When the ads come in, don't forget to optimize them for your site. It's very simple and will have a massive effect on your CTR, even at this early stage.

And that's all there is to it, apart from the final step... spending the money! I don't think you need my help for that, do you?

Part
2

Beyond Basic Ads

8. CATCH FICKLE VISITORS WITH THE GOOGLE SEARCH BOX

8.1 Finding Money With Search

What happens when your visitors can't find what they want on your website? They might be bored, probably they're hungry for more or they might want to refine their search. If you have a Google Search Box, you can now retain these 'quitters' — and make money from ads they click from their search results!

The Google Search Box isn't just an added convenience for your visitors — it can actually make you money! **When your users enter a search term, you'll receive a commission for any ad they click on the results page.**

If your AdSense ads are being ignored then, add a link at the bottom of the AdSense ads, inviting visitors to try Google search. A simple note should do the trick. Try something like: "Can't find what you're looking for? Try Google Search!"

A Google Search box allows your visitors to specify their exact search terms, thereby "pulling" more relevant ads to your page. Using the Search feature, you can pull up **on-demand AdSense ads** at the top of the search results.

> At the bottom of the Google text ads, place a link to the Google Search bar, inviting readers to Search for better-targeted content and offers. When visitors click an ad, YOU get paid!

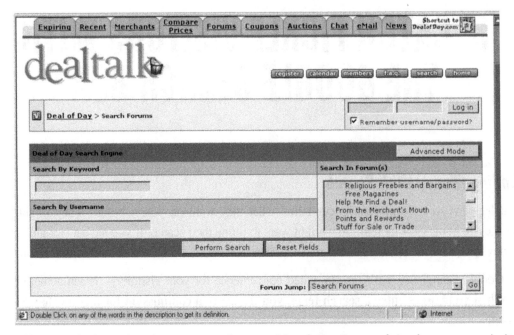

Fig 8.1 The "Search" feature is an important part of content-rich websites. On my website above, users are invited to search different threads within the website 'by keyword' and 'by username' creating a good potential to merge in a Google search box.

Google Search Boxes are getting increasingly popular with Internet Forums, enabling users to pull up relevant text ads "on demand"!

8.2 Learn How To Add Google Search To Your Web Page

Adding Google Search to your Web page is very easy. Click the "Get Ads" link under the AdSense Setup tab and you'll be offered six different types of AdSense products that you can place on your site:

- **AdSense for Content** — The graphic ads, text ad and link units discussed in the previous section.
- **AdSense for Search** — More than just a search box, AdSense for Search lets you build your own search engine related to your site's topic.
- **AdSense for Feeds** — Place ads in RSS feeds.
- **AdSense for Domains** — Place AdSense on sites you haven't even built yet!
- **Video Units** — Take content from YouTube and earn from the ads embedded into the videos.
- **AdSense for Mobile Content** — Use ads specially formatted for sites adapted for mobile devices.

Don't worry about all of these different products for now. I'll discuss them all in good time and explain how you can get the most out of each of them. To place a Google search box on your site though just click the AdSense for Search link.

Then you'll need to click again.

Clicking that link won't take you directly to the code for Google's search box. It will take you to a landing page with a neat little video that introduces AdSense for Search.

The reason is the AdSense for Search has changed quite a bit since it was first introduced.

When I first started using AdSense for Search, I saw it as little more than a way for users to leave a little money in the tip jar on their way out.

Now it's so much more than that.

The degree of customization, the options available and the control you can have over the results all mean that your search box is no longer a way out of your website.

It can be a guide to the rest of your Web pages too.

8.3 Your Sites... Or The World Wide Web

Hit the "Continue" button at the bottom of the landing page and you'll have to go through three stages before you're given your code.

The first choice you'll have to make is perhaps the hardest. You'll have to decide whether users will be searching the Web or only searching a list of sites that you've chosen.

In general, you'll only want them to search a list of sites that you've chosen. And ideally, you'll want all of those sites to be yours. That will make it more likely that you'll keep your users on your pages.

Obviously, that might not be possible initially. Everyone starts with just one site so when you first begin building websites, you'll only have one address that you can place in the list of selected sites.

But that's fine too. It gives your site a search function.

Anyone who uses that search function will only be searching your site. If they can't find what you're looking for — and the more you limit the range of sites that users can search, the greater the chances that they won't find what they want in the results — the more likely they are to click one of the ads that appear next to the results, earning you income.

If you want give your users a greater range of sites to search though, one option is to look at the options that other sites in your field provide. Ask them to add your site to their search engine in return for adding their site to yours. You'll have created an effective and highly targeted traffic exchange system.

There is a downside to this approach though. If users know that searching on your site will only bring them results related to your site's topic, they'll head directly to Google if they want to search for anything else.

If they'd searched from your site and clicked an ad, you would have got paid.

Google does allow you to place two AdSense for Search boxes on one page, but I think that's just confusing. Users won't know which box to use for what purpose.

The best solution is to begin by allowing users to search the Web and track your results. Then limit them to just your site or a group of related sites and track the results again.

You'll soon know which approach delivers the best revenues.

8.4 Flavoring Your Search Results

The next decision is even easier. You can also add keywords that help Google to deliver relevant results — and relevant ads.

So if you have a site about music, adding a list of music-related keywords means that someone tossing "bass" into your search box is more likely to get results about guitars than singing fish.

That's an option you'll definitely want to use!

8.5 Customizing Your Search Box

The next option looks like a head-scratcher. Google lets you customize your search in six different ways.

That's a trap. Don't touch a thing.

As far as possible, **use a staid gray button for the Google search feature and keep it exactly as Google provides it**. It looks more believable — and legitimate! Note that Google has not played around with its own search buttons, although the logo itself has undergone many theme-based transformations.

8.6 Search Results Have Style!

The next bunch of options are much harder. You'll have to decide where you want the results page to appear.

You have three choices:

- On a Google page in the same window;
- On a Google page in a new window;
- **On a page on your website**.

Clearly, the last option is the best; it gives you many more may ways to customize the page. You'll be given two codes: one for the search box and one for the results. You'll need to paste the search box code in the appropriate location on your Web page. The search results code goes on a page that you'll have to create specially to hold the results.

Not only will you be able to offer your users a search option and earn from the ads that appear on that page, you'll also be able to show your own internal links and AdSense ads to keep them on your site.

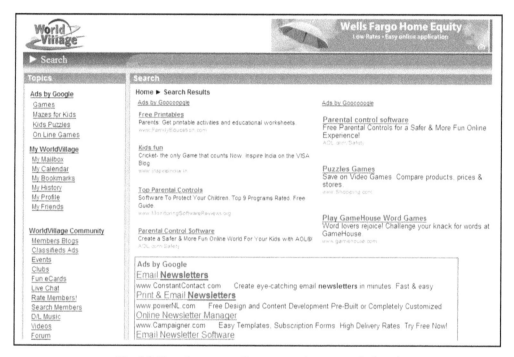

Fig. 8.2 Users have to scroll past an entire screen of ads and
links to reach the search results at WorldVillage.com.

You'll then be asked where you want the ads to appear, and again, you'll have three options:

- Top and Right
- Top and Bottom
- Right

The correct answer is… top and right. This is how the ads appear on Google's own search results and while you can sometimes find ads at the bottom of the page, not everyone gets all the way down there. You want the ads to be prominent all the time so make sure there are some at the top of the page and others on the side of the page, visible as they browse.

And finally, you'll be able to customize the ads themselves.

You should be familiar with this by now… you should know what you need to do. The links need to be blue and the text should match the text of the search results. If you're using a page of your own to display the results, try formatting the ads to match any links you might have in a sidebar. That will make the ads like part of your site's navigation.

And that's it! You'll then be given your code and you'll be free to earn from search on your site.

8.7 To Search Or Not To Search

Putting a Google search box on your site brings advantages and disadvantages. The big plus is that all the ads the user sees are going to be relevant. The user chooses the keyword so the results are going to be right in line with what the user wants.

On the other hand, that means you've got no control over the keywords they choose so you can't try to promote high-paying keywords. You have to take what you're given. You could have a high clickthrough rate but low revenues (although there's still no guarantee that the user will click on an ad rather than an unpaid listing on the search results page.)

But your users will leave your site at some point anyway. Why shouldn't you try to make money when they do click away? Even if search doesn't bring you huge amounts of money, you should still use it as an added revenue source and to bring extra functionality to your users.

8.8 Home Page Searching

One way to increase your revenues from searching is to encourage your users to use your site as their home page.

Many users have Google as their home page. If you're offering the same service as Google, using their search box and delivering their results, there's no reason why they shouldn't be searching from your page — and giving you revenue from the ads.

Just encourage your users, especially users with Google as their home page, to switch to you, and you'll be able to make the most of your search function and your ads.

9. BECOME A COMMISSION SELLER WITH AFFILIATE PROGRAMS

Google does great work but sometimes even Google gets things wrong. In the summer of 2008, Google announced that it was shutting down its referral program.

I doubt that many people noticed.

The idea, when it launched, was good. In addition to paying for impressions and for clicks, advertisers could also choose to pay for specific actions taken by users such as making a purchase, signing up for a newsletter or downloading a program or ebook.

Instead of paying for leads, they'd only be paying for conversions. And because those users would be so valuable, the companies would be willing to pay publishers more than the cents or dollar or two that they might pay for a click. They may even agree to pay a percentage of the sales price, an amount that could generate a handsome income.

It wasn't a new idea, of course. Publishers have been signing up for affiliate programs on the Web forever using exactly this model. But Google's giant inventory of advertisers meant that it should have been able to dominate the market, making it easy for affiliate advertisers and publishers to find each other.

It didn't happen. In part, that was because Google began by promoting its own products, paying for referrals to AdSense — which would only have appealed to sites directed at other publishers who would have known about the service anyway — and for downloads of its image-editing software Picassa. The payments just weren't high enough to persuade publishers to give up valuable advertising real estate on their pages.

When it came to roll out a referral program that allowed any publisher to offer deals, publishers were already skeptical. The system itself was complex and publishers were already used to working with DoubleClick, the market leader.

So Google bought DoubleClick for an incredible $3.1 billion and closed its own referral program.

Publishers that were using the old referral program found that they were no longer showing ads and were directed to Google's new Affiliate Network at www.google.com/ads/affiliatenetwork instead which was based on DoubleClick's system.

It's worth looking at and in this chapter, I'm going to explain why and how you should be using affiliate ads alongside your AdSense units.

9.1 Pay-Per-Click, Cost-Per-Mille And Cost-Per-Action... Three Complementary Ways To Monetize Your Site

The challenge for every Internet publisher is to turn as many of their users into cash as possible.

For sites that sell products directly, that's usually going to mean persuading visitors to make a purchase in exactly the same way that any store needs to generate sales.

For sites that only provide content though, it means advertising and there are three ways to do that online.

Ads that pay on a CPM basis allow publishers to earn from every user... even if they only earn a cent or a fraction of a cent for each one.

Ads that pay on a CPC basis allow publishers to earn from the users that are of most interest to advertisers. Publishers may only earn from 3-4 percent of their users but the amounts they earn for each click can quickly add up.

And affiliate ads that pay a commission for each sale may only be paid for a tiny fraction of a site's users but can amount to tens and even hundreds of dollars for each payment.

Each of these approaches complements the others. With a CPM program, you'll earn for every user. The CPC program will allow you to make *additional* income from some of those users. And the affiliate program will allow you to make even more money from those who actually buy.

You can think of integrating these different methods as covering your site's exits with three levels of nets to catch as much money as possible. If you don't earn from one system, you'll earn from another.

9.2 Google's Affiliate Network

There are all sorts of different affiliate networks available on the Web. Some are small, some are big and some are just giants. Some only work with large publishers while others are happy to take on anyone who knocks on their door.

Publishers have reported plenty of success with Commission Junction (www.cj.com) and LinkShare (www.linkshare.com) but for me, there are two that really stand out.

The first is Google's Affiliate Network, which you can find at www.google.com/ads/affiliatenetwork.

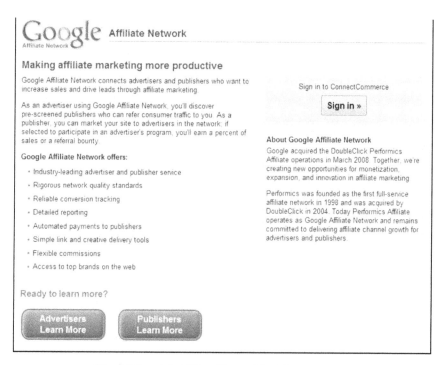

Fig. 9.1 Google's Affiliate Network isn't for everyone...

Although the system looks very much like AdSense — and the interface is as easy to use — there are some major differences between Google's Affiliate Network and its pay-per-click ads.

For one, unlike AdWords, the Affiliate Betwork won't take any old advertiser. Advertisers have to apply, be interviewed by a Google representative... and pay $2,000.

Half of that $2,000 is an advance on the payments that advertisers have to pay to publishers. That's good news. It means that advertisers can't sign up, enjoy a month of free sales then disappear without paying their advertisers' commissions.

The other $1,000 is a non-refundable service fee that pays to set up the account. And advertisers have to agree to pay a minimum of $500 in commissions every month... whether their publishers generate $500 worth of commissions or not.

All of that means that the kinds of ads you see on the Google Affiliate Network are going to come from decent-sized, established companies.

That's a big advantage but perhaps the biggest advantage of using this system is that it comes from Google. It's simple to use, you know you're dealing with a reputable company and you can be sure that you'll get paid.

9.3 Become An Amazon Associate

Another big, trusted company with an affiliate program is Amazon.com. Amazon prefers to call its affiliates "associates," which makes them sound more like sales staff than independent publishers hoping to get paid for recommending products, but it amounts to the same thing.

You can sign up, help yourself to a huge range of different types of ads for a giant range of products, earning up to 15 percent of the sales price.

That commission is actually relatively low. It is certainly possible to find merchants willing to pay half the sales price to affiliates, and Amazon actually caps the commissions on some high-priced goods. But the advantages of using Amazon may well outweigh the low payments.

The range of products is so broad that you shouldn't have any problem finding a product that fits your site exactly, and because just about everyone has already bought something at Amazon, they'll feel comfortable using the site to make their purchase.

That's a huge advantage over other sellers who will be demanding the user's credit card details.

You can sign up for Amazon's affiliate program at affiliate-program.amazon.com. Just be sure to choose ad formats that match the position you want to place the ads and blend them into your page.

Fig. 9.2 AmazonAssociates lets anyone earn from the online retailer.

9.4 How To Really Make Money With An Affiliate Program

You could write an entire book on making money with affiliate programs, and plenty of people have. But generating the kinds of clicks that translate into commissions isn't difficult and there's no great secret. You just have to:

- **Make recommendations.**

  Place a random affiliate unit on a Web page and it just looks like another ad. Recommend that your readers buy that product and there's a good chance that many of them will.

  After all, they trust you so when they read that you've used the product and recommend that they do too, they'll feel confident that they're not wasting their money.

  You can't do this with AdSense units. But because affiliates ads only pay if someone buys, merchants actually want you to recommend the items they're selling.

  Talk them up in your content. Write reviews. Add affiliate links every time you mention a product that has benefitted you. It's the best way to ensure that you get sales.

- **Choose good products that you can endorse personally.**

  But that means you have to choose your products very, very carefully. Because you're giving your word that the item is worth buying, if it turns out to be a bad buy, your users will blame you.

  They'll stop trusting you, they'll stop visiting your site and they certainly won't click on any more affiliate links.

  They'll also tell other people not to visit your site too.

  Only recommend products that you know are worth the money.

  If that means not having an affiliate ad on the page, that's fine. It's better than having an affiliate ad that harms your site.

  In fact, that often means that the best place to look for affiliate ads isn't Google or Amazon. It's on your bookshelves, in your toolbox and among the people you know.

  Choose products that you already trust instead of looking for items to promote and you'll find them much easier to recommend.

10. USING MULTIPLE AD BLOCKS

Google lets you place more than one ad unit on each page of your Web site. In fact, you can place:

3 ad units

3 link units

2 AdSense for search boxes

1 AdSense for video unit

What does this mean for web publishers?

A real bonanza: you now have many more chances to hook readers with new ads as Google will show unique ads in each ad unit!

With multiple ad blocks, you can also decide which ads are served in the best places for your site.

10.1 How Many Ads Is Too Many?

In general, I recommend that you put as many AdSense units on your page as possible. The more choices you give your users, the more likely they are to click.

The only caveat to this is ad-blindness. Put lots of ads on your site and users are just going to ignore them. And when they ignore one unit, they're likely to ignore them all.

This can be more of a problem for small Web pages than for larger pages such as those on blogs. On a short page, all those different ads can quickly outweigh the content; on a long page, you can scatter them about so that they're less likely to get in the way of a user's reading.

One great solution is to have a long home page with lots of ads but which contains only the headlines and the first paragraph or so from each article. To read more, the user has to click to a page with just that one article.

That page would have fewer units. But because those units would be influenced by just one article, the ads would be better targeted.

10.2 What To Do With Three Ad Units

The actual number of ads that you'll choose will depend on the design of your site. But considering the range of different formats, you should find it pretty easy to squeeze in at least two ad units and usually three.

Most sites for example, have room for a leaderboard (although you should also experiment with a link unit to see which of the two in that position gives you the best results).

It's also not too difficult to insert a rectangular unit into an article. You can do that with just about any article.

That's two units already.

The final unit, a button or vertical banner, could do very well in a sidebar.

Most people choose to keep the ads far apart, but you can also have some pretty dramatic effects by putting your ad units together. This isn't a strategy that's going to work for everyone, but creating a zone — at the top of your page maybe or between blog entries — can really make those ads look like content.

After all, users are used to seeing ads in single blocks. When they see a whole section of the page given over to ads, there's a good chance they'll assume it's content and give it some extra attention.

10.3 Where To Put The Search Boxes

The search boxes are usually easier. Probably the most popular place for these is one of the top corners or in the sidebar.

You could try putting the second one at the bottom of the page if you want to give users somewhere to go when they've finished reading, but to be frank, I doubt if you'll make any more money with a search box down there than you would from the one at the top.

They're a good way to capture revenue from users who don't click on the ads and are about to leave, but I don't think that putting two search boxes on a page is going to give you more income than one. It's possible and you can try it. But I wouldn't expect any massive results.

10.4 Google Is Generous With The Link Units

Two search boxes might not make much of a difference, but I think that three link units might. They're small enough to squeeze into all sorts of spots and they look so good at the top and bottom of a list of links that you could probably have fun with three of them.

You do want to be careful about not overloading your page with so many ads that users stop seeing them, so if you don't have space for all three use just one or two.

And because link units look very different to ad units, I don't think you have to worry too much about them competing for clicks — and ending up with nothing. They go very well with other ad units.

10.5 Put Affiliate Ads Near The Recommendation

Affiliate ads work will in all sorts of places. Amazon's units tend to stand out pretty well, especially when they contain an image and can function effectively on the side of the page.

Often though, the best way to earn from an affiliate ad is to use a link in the text of the article the first time you mention it. You can't get better embedding than that!

10.6 Putting It All Together

Deciding where to put one ad can often be difficult. There are so many different options. Get it wrong and it will cost you money.

While having multiple ads lets you tempt users wherever they are on the page, it also compounds the problem. What's the best combination of ads and where should the different ads go?

Experimentation and close tracking is the only real way to know for your site but you have to start somewhere. I've put three suggested starting points below. These aren't meant to be final versions that will yield you the greatest income. They're just meant to get you started quickly. You can then try swapping the locations of different units and see how those changes affect your CTR.

10.7 Putting Multiple Ads In Articles

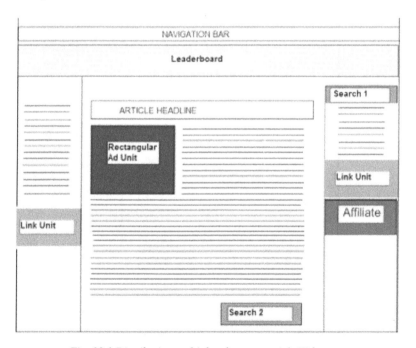

Fig. 10.1 Distributing multiple ads on an article Web page.

On a Web page that features just one article, you could place a leaderboard beneath the navigation bar, a rectangular ad unit embedded at the beginning of the article and a link unit in a list of links in the left-hand sidebar.

On the right, you could place a search box, another link list (perhaps to archives, RSS content or news) followed by a link unit, and you could put a graphic affiliate ad directly beneath the link unit to draw the reader's eye to the right and towards the link unit.

You could also try a second search box at the bottom of the page.

Possible alternatives to try:

- Swapping the leaderboard or the second search box for a link unit;
- Replacing the link unit on the left with a vertical banner;
- Placing a half-banner at the end of the article instead of the second search box;
- Moving the link unit on the left to the top of the sidebar;
- Using a skyscraper on the right instead of a link unit;
- Adding a text affiliate link to the article;
- Or just taking out some of the ads to see if that brings in more clicks.

10.8 Putting Multiple Ads In Blogs

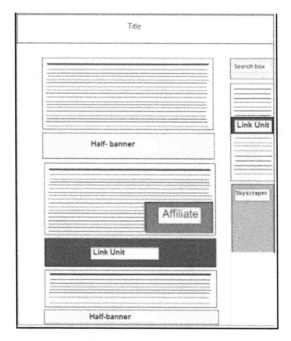

Fig. 10.2 Distributing multiple ads on a blog.

The best places to put ads on a blog is between the blog entries. Link units would probably be ideal here... but you could also start with a half-banner or even a full banner and use a link unit in between two of the blog entries.

A search button can be placed at the top of a sidebar on the right with a skyscraper blended into the second of two lists of links, and a second link unit between them. The referral unit can be placed inside one of the blog posts if the teaser is long enough and the product mentioned.

Possible alternatives to try:

- Swapping the link unit for another ad unit and using a link unit in place of the skyscraper;
- Using banners instead of half-banners;
- Embedding a rectangular ad unit into the text of the blog;
- Placing ad units next to photos in the blogs;
- Putting an affiliate ad in the sidebar;
- Adding an extra search box to the bottom of the right-hand sidebar.

10.9 Putting Multiple Ads In Merchant Sites

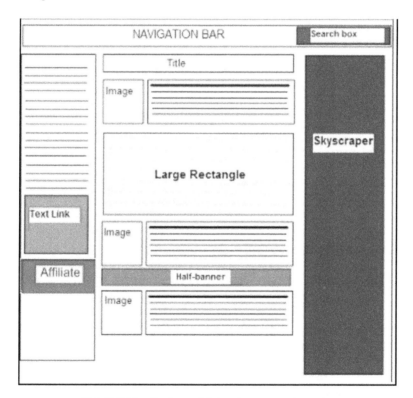

Fig. 10.3 Distributing multiple ads on a merchant site.

There are really two approaches you can take to using AdSense on merchant sites. The first is simply to treat them in the same way as blogs: put a link at the end of each section of advertising copy and place a banner or half banner beneath it. That ad unit should blend into the text above and below. You can use a skyscraper on the edge of the screen, a link unit beneath a list of navigation links, a search box at the top of the page and affiliate ads on the side.

Alternatively, you could use graphic affiliate ads as images and write text about the products. That would give you an instant online store!

In the sample layout above, I've placed a large rectangular ad unit directly beneath a featured product. The feature would create the most attention and users would have read past it to reach the rest of the page.

Whenever you're using AdSense on merchant sites though do keep a close eye on the ads you're serving; you don't want to advertise your competitors!

Possible alternatives to try:

- Using a text link instead one of the ad units between the marketing copy;
- Placing a large picture of a product on a page... and an ad unit right next to it;
- Using banners instead of half-banners;
- Placing a leaderboard either at the top of the page or at the bottom;
- Separating each piece of marketing copy with a large square unit.

And if you're worried you've put in too many ad units... just take one out and see if your CTR changes.

10.10 Ordering Your Ads

These strategies make for useful default placements. But there's one more factor that you should consider when you're planning your ads: the way that Google distributes ads to multiple units on a page.

The first ad unit to appear on a Web page always shows the ads that placed the highest bids. In other words, **the higher an ad appears on a page, the more that ad is worth.**

Because ads that are above the fold tend to get more clicks than those lower down the page, you won't usually have to do a thing to make sure that the ads that receive the most clicks are those that pay the most.

If your channels do show you that an ad unit at the bottom of the page is picking up more clicks than ad unit at the top of the page though, you might want try moving that unit to a higher position.

Frankly, I doubt that's going to happen very often. A bigger problem is if you've placed your ad units inside DIV tags, tables or other positioning codes. As far as AdSense is concerned, the first ad unit is the first one the robot comes across in the HTML code, even if that HTML code places the unit at the bottom of the page.

When you place multiple ad units on a Web page then, it's important to make sure that the AdSense codes appear in your HTML in the same order that they appear on your Web page. That should ensure that the ad units with the highest clickthrough rates are always the ones with the highest value ads.

11. BUILDING CONTENT

11.1 Writing Content

AdSense works better than just about every other type of online advertising for one simple reason: the ads are relevant to the content on your page. Users click on the ads because they find them interesting.

And they come back and click on them *again* because they find your content interesting.

If your site doesn't have good content, you're going to struggle to attract users and links, and you won't be able to persuade anyone to come back to your site.

Having the right content then is crucial to earning good revenues with AdSense. It's also crucial to the relationship you have with Google's indexing mechanism. Remember, Google is a search engine first and foremost. Its purpose is to provide Web users with the best search results for the terms they are seeking. If you are providing quality content, you have a greater chance of seeing your site come up higher on the search results page.

Fortunately, it's also easier than ever to fill your site with page after page of sticky content, each of which contains ad units and opportunities to earn revenue.

The most obvious way to create content is of course to **write it yourself**. Pick a subject you like and pour your heart out. If you know everything there is to know about video games, you could set up a site stuffed with reviews, news and walkthroughs, and write all the articles yourself. Your AdSense units will give you ads related to gaming and as long as they're positioned properly and look right they should give you more than enough revenue to fund your video gaming habit and then some. You can do the same thing for any topic you wanted.

But remember, if you've created your site to make money, then writing the content yourself means that you're *working* for that money. When you count your revenues, you have to factor in the time and effort it took you to make that revenue.

That's one of the reasons that many people look for other, easier ways to get content around their ads. (The fact that they just don't like writing is another good reason.) Fortunately, there are plenty of ways of creating relatively effortless content and some of them are even free.

11.2 Making Bucks With Blogs

Writing blogs isn't exactly effortless, but it is something a lot of people do for fun, and because they're updated regularly, Google loves them. If you're going to write a blog anyway, then you should certainly be making money out of it.

The biggest challenge when writing a blog is getting ads that give you good revenues. Because your entries are going to be talking about all sorts of different things, there's a chance that you're going to get ads on all sorts of random topics.

That's fine, unless your ads are barely giving you enough revenue to pay for the blog.

If you find that you're getting lots of ads related to "blogs" for example, instead of what you're blogging about, you can try changing the meta name in your template. Delete the <$Metainfodata$> tag and replace it with your own keywords and description:

```
<meta name="robots" content="index,follow">
<meta name="keywords" Content="Your keywords">
<meta name="description" Content="Keyword-rich description">
```

Make sure that your blog has plenty of keywords and use lots of headlines containing key phrases, repeating them throughout the blog.

Above all though, make sure that your blog has plenty of text. It might be fun to stuff your pages with pictures of friends, family and pets but Google can't read them and you'll end up with public service ads instead of revenue.

11.3 Adding AdSense To Your Blog

Not all blog sites use the same template so how you add AdSense to your blog will depend on the company you're using.

For users of Blogger.com, which is owned by Google, one option is put the ads in the template section of the site:

```
<!-- Begin .post -->
<div class="post"><a name="<$BlogItemNumber$>"></a>
<BlogItemTitle>
<h3 class="post-title">
<BlogItemUrl><a href="<$BlogItemUrl$>" title="external link"></BlogItemUrl>
<$BlogItemTitle$>
```

```
<BlogItemUrl></a></BlogItemUrl>
</h3>
</BlogItemTitle>
<!--Your AdSense code -->
```

For example, crayfish-info.blogspot.com puts ads directly above the text. The ads are centered above the <div> tag and he's added a <br> break tag to add a gap between the head and Google, and help his ads to stand out.

To do the same thing to your blogspot blog, click "Change Settings" on the Dashboard and then click "Template Tab." Somewhere on the page, below the CSS material, you should find a section of code that begins:

```
<p id="description"><$BlogDescription$></p>
</div></div><br>
```

The code should then look like this:

```
...............................................<div align="center">
<script type="text/javascript"><!--
google_ad_client = "pub-xxxxx09818xxxxx";
google_ad_width = 728;
google_ad_height = 90;
google_ad_format = "728x90_as";
google_ad_channel ="117893460x";
google_ad_type = "text_image";
google_color_border = "336666";
google_color_bg = "669966";
google_color_link = "CCFF99";
google_color_url = "003333";
google_color_text = "FFFFFF";
//--></script>
<script type="text/javascript"
  src="http://pagead2.googlesyndication.com/pagead/show_ads.js">
</script></center></div>
<!-- Begin #main — Contains main-column blog content -->
```

Before uploading, check the preview to make sure that the ads are where and how you want them, then "Save Template Changes" and "Republish" to refresh the blog.

Of course, you don't have to place AdSense directly above the text. **Another option is to embed the ads** *within* **the text so that they appear after particular entries.** That would limit you to three entries per page (if you wanted an ad unit after each entry) but it could increase your clickthroughs.

Blogger lets you do this automatically. Click the Layout tab, then the Page Elements link and finally, Edit in the Blog Posts section. You'll find a check box that lets you show ads between posts on the home page.

You'll even be able to format the ads from that same control panel, making the whole process very, very simple.

11.4 Old Content

Blogs have to be written all the time, but if you've ever written anything in the past, don't just let it gather dust on your shelf. Give your old work a new lease of life by throwing it onto the Web!

For example, "Low Fat Linux" by Bob Rankin was written years ago. You may be able to find it on Amazon.com, but it's not likely that many people are buying it because you can read the entire book for free at www.lowfatlinux.com.

Bob's content has done its job of selling copies. Now it's doing a second job, selling clicks to ads.

What have you got lying around that could be earning you money?

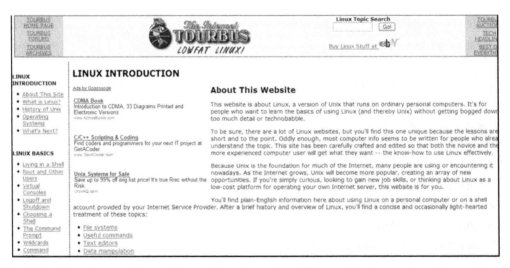

Fig. 11.1 Bob Rankin makes money from old notes. Note the position of his ads. They're prominent but could he get more clicks by putting them on the right? He could also have added an AdLink unit above the list of links on the left.

You might have an ebook of your own that isn't selling very well. Instead of attempting to sell your ebook for $19.95, why not turn it into Web pages and make it available for free for all to enjoy? Paste your AdSense code on the pages and you may make more from the ads than from sales of your ebook. Repurposing old content is a fantastic way to draw water from your own well.

I did this with a book that I'd written about online dating. The home page contains a list of chapter headings with a skyscraper ad on the left and a Google search box beneath it. There's also a banner on the top, which I expect people largely to ignore. That ad does however make the ad unit look less commercial and the text ads match the list of chapter headings (although I used red for the links to match the color scheme of the page).

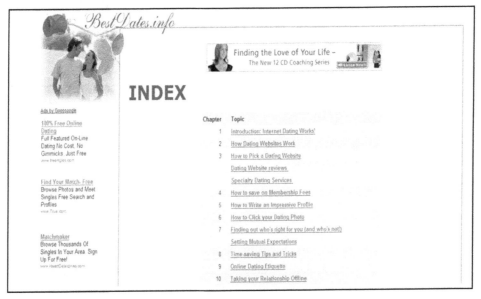

Fig. 11.2 BestDates.info — Making money by using old content to bring people together.

Note that this is a professional-looking website. That's important. The fact that you're using old content is no excuse for using an old design. You still have to make the page look good and pick up high-quality traffic if you want to get the clicks and the revenues.

On the internal pages, I've pushed the ads a little harder. Above the fold, there's little real content and a lot ads. To stop people from scrolling away immediately though, I've used a nice big picture. I know that users will stop to look at that image. They'll then look at the ads and only after they've done that will they scroll down to read the page.

I've also put a long list of links on the left under the skyscraper to help the ads blend in and placed a third unit at the bottom of the page next to the free download.

Fig. 11.3 Ads and an image above the fold at BestDates.info

And the best thing about this strategy is that I've got so many pages of content to use. Each page is a separate chance to capture more clicks. I could even spin off the content on those pages and market them as individual articles or websites.

11.5 Volunteer Writers

To use old content, you have to have the pages in the first place. If you don't happen to have any out-of-print books that you've written lying around — and you don't feel like writing something new — another option is to ask people to write for your site for free.

Lots of people like writing. Just look at Amazon. They didn't pay a penny for all those book reviews. Their users write them for free and Amazon benefits.

When I started WorldVillage.com, I didn't have money to pay the people who reviewed software for me. Instead, I contacted the game companies and received complimentary copies of their computer games, which I then forwarded to a staff of volunteer writers. The agreement was that they would provide me with a written review of the game and they would keep the game as payment. I've got dozens of game reviews that bring users to my site and get them clicking on my ads. I didn't pay a penny for them but years later they continue to generate revenue for me.

You don't have to use reviews though. Whatever the subject of your website, you can add a line asking people to send in their thoughts and comments. You can just say something like: "We want YOU! We want your thoughts, articles and comments. Send your submissions to editor@yoursite.com and we'll post them here."

You can then create a whole new set of pages for your users' submissions and put AdSense on each one of them.

Fig. 11.4 Game reviews at www.worldvillage.com/softwarereviews/index.html
Mmm... free content.

11.6 Build Thousands of Pages with Other People's Content

What is the focus of your web site? Is it all about parenting? Do you help people with their finances? Does your newsletter introduce people to new web sites? Or is your focus on the legal field? Regardless of your niche, you can benefit from taking advantage of one of the little-known secrets of AdSense experts... FREE syndicated articles.

Many writers want nothing more than to have their work published and read. Syndicated content is a dream-come-true for writers AND publishers. For the writer, it exposes their work to a larger audience. And for the publisher (that's you!), it means more quality content for your site. You might not be aware that there are literally THOUSANDS of articles available online which you can easily add to your web site!

Of course, the trick is knowing where to find these articles. Below is a list that can get you started by showing you where you can find over 30,000 articles that are ready to be placed on your own web site.

Please note that each site has its own restrictions and rules for using its content. In all cases, you must leave the author's name and web site link intact. Some sites require that you also link back to the site where you found the article. This is critical! Remember that while you are allowed to use the articles on your pages, the content is still property of the author. Please give credit where credit is due!

You may wish to publish articles only relevant to your topic, or you may wish to become a publishing powerhouse, adding thousands of new pages to your site. Regardless of how you wish to approach it, here are a few sites that provide you with thousands of FREE articles that you can republish on your web sites.

EzineArticles.com

www.ezinearticles.com

A gigantic resources featuring over 150,000 writers covering a huge range of topics. However, they do have a limit of 25 articles/year for each site and many of the articles are worth what you pay for them. Look through the categories and you can select some gems but be prepared to spend a lot of time sifting.

DotComWomen.com

www.dotcomwomen.com/free-content.shtml

A nice selection of articles targeting women.

John Watson

members.tripod.com/buckcreek

John offers his stories for site owners to enjoy and place on their sites.

ValuableContent.com

www.valuablecontent.com

Like eZineArticles, ValuableContent.com offers dozens of categories with hundreds of articles for you to publish. This resource though charges contributors $9.99 per month to submit their articles. That means a small range of articles to choose from but better quality content.

Patricia Fripp

www.fripp.com/articleslist.html

Patricia Fripp is a businesswoman, marketer and motivational speaker. Her site offers over one hundred articles perfect for any business-oriented site.

ArticleCity.com

www.articlecity.com

This one is a source of articles that will keep you busy for weeks on end. ArticleCity offers over 12,000 articles that you can place on your site. If the topic exists, you can bet that this site will have an article on it. I recommend spending a great deal of time selecting articles for your site here.

Want to find more? Simply do a Google search for "free articles" and see what turns up. Fine tune your search for your topic to find articles relevant to your site, such as "free parenting articles" or "free financial articles."

Now that you know where to find free content, you can build hundreds or thousands of keyword relevant pages and place your AdSense code on them to generate more revenue.

11.7 Add Public Domain Works To Your Site

One of the best kept secrets of free content comes in the form of Public Domain works. These are books, articles, recordings and pictures whose copyrights have expired. Since they have not been re-registered with a copyright, they enter the public domain. What does that mean? It means ANYONE (including you) can publish, re-publish and/or sell the works without paying a commission to anyone!

You can build a site with HUNDREDS of pages just by publishing one public domain book on your site! Think of all the AdSense impressions you can deliver. The possibilities are endless.

I have two sources that you will want to investigate to find Public Domain works that you can begin using immediately

Idea #1 — Project Gutenberg

Project Gutenberg is the oldest producer of free electronic books on the Internet. Their collection of more than 27,000 eBooks was produced by hundreds of volunteers. As of this writing, the top 10 most popular works on Project Gutenberg are:

- *The Outline of Science, Vol. 1 (of 4)* by J. Arthur Thomson
- *Manners, Customs, and Dress During the Middle Ages and During the Renaissance Period* by P. L. Jacob
- *Illustrated History of Furniture* by Frederick Litchfield
- *The Kama Sutra of Vatsyayana* by Vatsyayana
- *Pride and Prejudice* by Jane Austen
- *Searchlights on Health* by B. G. Jefferis and J. L. Nichols
- *History of the United States* by Charles A. Beard and Mary Ritter Beard
- *Our Day* by William Ambrose Spicer
- *The Adventures of Huckleberry Finn* by Mark Twain
- *The People's Common Sense Medical Adviser in Plain English* by Ray Vaughn Pierce

Check out their entire library at **www.gutenberg.org**.

Please note that while you may republish these works on your site, you are not allowed to resell the works themselves.

The downside of using works from Project Gutenberg is that hundreds of other people may already be using them. You might opt for less popular works in order to get better search engine placement.

Idea #2 – Public Domain Riches

Very few people have mastered the art of turning public domain works into cash like Yanik Silver. Yanik has made a ton of money with public domain and his course shows you how you can do the same.

From Yanik's Web page, here is what you will learn in Public Domain Riches…

The best places online (and off) to actually find public domain works. (I'll hand you over my best resources on a silver platter.)

- How to find a slew of public domain works in 3 minutes or less on just about any subject you want with just one click!
- How to determine exactly if a work is in the public domain. (Especially where to research if a work from 1923-1963 is really in the public domain. Remember, this is where the real bonanza of recent material can be found - but this can also be a dangerous "gray area" for many works if you're not careful).
- How to tap into the vast repositories of government publications. Yes, Uncle Sam publishes more content than anyone else and much of it is - can I hear the magic word again? - FREE!
- What to do if someone challenges your public domain claim.
- How to wade through the deliberately misleading copyright notices on many works that should really be public domain. (But on the flipside - you'll want to know how to look threatening so any "Two-bit Johnny" won't rip off the material you found in the public domain.)
- The 7 different ways to profitably use public domain info.
- How to quickly and easily put public domain works into a "saleable" format.
- The secret to modifying public domain works so they are exclusively yours alone and then selling them for hundreds of dollars!
- Yanik knows public domain, so you might want to check out Public Domain Riches at www. publicdomainriches.com/home.php?40271

11.8 Buying Content/ Hiring Writers

One of the problems with free content is that you can get what you pay for. And if your site doesn't have valuable content, it's going to have an effect on your clickthroughs.

The alternative of course is to pay professional writers to write for you. I've already mentioned Elance (www.elance.com) as a good place to find designers but it's a good place to find writers too. You can also ask ConstantConversions.com (www.ConstantConversions.com) to write articles and blog posts for you.

The advantage of hiring writers of course, is that you can be sure you're getting good content with little effort. On the other hand, you have to make that money back.

Try testing a writer to see how much profit a series of articles generates. If you pay $200 for five articles but find that your new pages don't give you a $200 increase in revenues, you either need a new idea — or a new writer.

There are a couple of cheaper options though.

The first is to use Scribat.com (www.scribat.com). This is a relatively new service — the Beta launched at the beginning of 2009 — and it aims to help publishers in two ways. You can tell them what kind of content you need and how often you need it, and they'll match your site to a writer (or a team of writers) and handle the content creation for you. All you'll have to do is approve it, paste it and monetize it.

Alternatively, Scribat also encourages its writers to submit articles for syndication. You'll pay as little as $9.95 for the right to reprint one of the articles and you'll be free to place ads alongside it and keep the revenues for yourself. The only downside is that the article may appear on other websites but it will be up to your marketing skills to ensure that users come to your site and not someone else's.

If you can't find an article on the site that you can use, just drop them a line and ask them if they have any content that suits you. Scribat will then issue a callout to the writers to submit their posts.

It's a very easy way to pick up some high-quality, low-cost content.

Another option is to encourage writers to submit articles to your site yourself, on a revenue-sharing basis.

Again, there are a couple of ways that you can do this.

The first is to include the writer's own AdSense code in the body of his or her text. So you could strike a deal with a writer who sends a couple of posts every week. You place your own AdSense units at the top and bottom of the post, and the writer's AdSense unit embedded in the text. Whoever gets the clicks gets the revenue.

That's one approach that Google recommends but I think that there's a better one.

All of the content at WorldVillage.com is submitted by freelance writers on a revenue-sharing basis. Again, we paste the writer's AdSense code onto the page but we also place our ads and instead of showing both types of ads all the time — so that they're competing — we run a neat little code that makes sure that each code is shown 50 percent of the time.

Each of us then ends up with half the revenue.

It's not a very complex piece of code and if you can't write it yourself, there are plenty of freelance programmers at Elance and Scriptlance who should be able to do it for you for no more than a few hundred bucks.

11.9 Automated Content

Another option you can use to build a website is automated content. This will let you cut through the hassle of creating a website from scratch, dreaming up content and driving traffic. For a fee, you'll be able to launch without delay a website that's filled with information and already optimized for search engines.

As long as your ads are bringing in more money than you're spending for the program, you're making a profit.

The folks at Google aren't crazy about pre-fabricated, useless content and it's unlikely your users will be either. If all you're doing is building a site to earn money — and not because you're genuinely interested in the subject of your site — then maybe it doesn't matter. You can still launch your pre-fabricated site, post your ads in good places and send traffic to your advertisers.

It's worth remembering though that Smart Pricing was introduced precisely because of sites like these: sites with low-quality content get low advertising prices. It's quite possible that having built your site, you'll find that the prices you receive will drop because you're not sending the advertisers users who are genuinely interested in their products.

The best way to ensure a high result from Smart Pricing is to give advertisers traffic that wants their product. Good content is the best way to do that.

If you are going to use pre-fabricated content though, then you can still try to keep the cost of your advertising space high by attracting good quality traffic. The users might not stay on your site for very long — and you don't really want them to — but if you can lay out your ads in such a way that when those users click off the site, they end up at an advertiser who does have the content they want to buy, you should still make money.

One thing you do have to be concerned about though is combining sites with pre-fabricated content in the same AdSense account as sites with high-quality content. If your Smart Pricing value does fall, then your income could fall across the board.

The best strategy if you're going to use these programs, I think, is to try to keep the sites you create with them in a separate account whenever possible, and just make sure that your income is always higher than any monthly fee.

On the whole though, you'll probably find that it's more enjoyable and more lucrative to create websites that you enjoy maintaining and that users like visiting. Those are the sort of sites that make the most money.

11.10 Google's Video Content

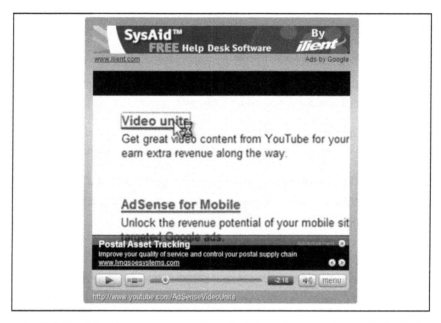

Fig. 11.5 Google's video content comes from YouTube and arrives with two kinds of ads.

One type of content that users love — and which you can pick up for free — is videos.

Users love them.

They watch television on YouTube and they've become used to seeing videos on blogs and websites. Even Oprah has her own YouTube channel.

That's both a challenge and an opportunity for publishers. It's a challenge because creating original video content can appear difficult and look expensive. Actually, it doesn't have to be either, although at the very least, you will need a digital camera.

And after putting together "The Next Internet Millionaire," I can tell you it's also a lot of fun!

But video is also an opportunity because you don't need original content. There are tons of clips available on the Web that you can place on your own site and earn from the ads on your page and embedded ads in the video itself.

Two of the best places to find videos like these are Revver and Google itself.

Revver doesn't have as big an inventory as YouTube, but it does share ad revenue. The site embeds an ad into the video, lets publishers place the clip on their own site and gives them 20 percent of the income. That might not sound like much, but don't forget, you're getting the content for free and you can still put AdSense units around it.

The alternative is to use Google's video content... which is drawn from YouTube.

The videos come with two different kinds of ads.

Text overlay ads target signals in the video and on the Web page to produce relevant ads that pay on a CPC basis. InVideo ads, used on YouTube clips, pay on a CPM basis.

Interestingly, the overlay ad changes as the film progresses and users can even choose to move back and forward through the ads. They can also choose to close the overlay, which might not be so good.

You can only place one video unit on a page but you can change the surrounding color to blend the unit into your site, choose from three different sizes and select content by category, creator or receive it automatically targeted to keywords you supply.

Here's how you do it:

You'll need to click the AdSense Setup tab in your AdSense account, then choose the link marked "Video units." Agree to the Terms and Conditions (after you've read them all very carefully, of course!) and you'll be taken directly to... YouTube.

If you already have a YouTube account, you'll be able to log in, and if you don't, you'll be able to sign up to receive one.

You'll then have to enter your AdSense Publisher ID details to confirm who you are and merge your AdSense account with your YouTube account.

The following steps are where it all gets a bit more fun. You'll now get to create your media player. There are a few points to watch out for here.

The first is that you have to give your media player a name and description.

These fields might look unnecessary but they can actually be very helpful. Make the descriptions meaningful and you'll be able to make useful comparisons to see which locations, optimizations and types of content yield the highest revenues.

That's always the key to successful ad-supported publishing.

So if you had a website about cars, for example, and wanted to run a weekly video, you could create one media player for NASCAR content and one about rally cars. Swap them after a week or so and you'll be to see which delivers the biggest rewards for you. And because you've marked the media player, choosing the one that will remain permanently on your pages should be very simple.

Next, you'll get to choose the player's color scheme.

Again, choose colors that help the player to blend into your site.

You might not have made these videos, but you want your users to feel that you did.

There's nothing wrong with that. Televisions stations do it every time they run syndicated shows. They don't hide the fact that someone else made the shows they're running but they don't announce it either.

Choose colors that match your site — and you've only got nine schemes to choose from — and not only will you have a better-looking Web page but you'll also be able to make the most of the trust your users have in your content.

A tougher choice is the size of media player to use. Google only offers three options here: mini, standard and full size.

My advice? Go for the standard. In general, big is best but the full size player also offers thumbnails that link to other videos. You won't be able to control all of those videos and when offered too much choice users might choose "none of the above."

Choose one for them and it looks like a recommendation. They're more likely to hit the Play button and generate the ads.

It's in the last option that things get really tough though.

When Google rolled out this plan, the company left a big hole.

It didn't allow publishers to choose the clips themselves.

That made publishers very unhappy especially when Google served automated video that wasn't very relevant.

There's still a hole in the plan.

You still can't pick your own ads. Instead, you can choose "Automated Content" which lets Google and YouTube analyze your site and decide what kind of videos to show. Adding keywords to the "Hints" box will help to make sure that your videos are relevant.

Alternatively, you can choose to take your ads by "Category/Provider." So the publisher of a car site could simply choose to take videos in the "car" category.

If you do want to choose the videos yourself though — and I think that's always the best approach — there is a way to do it.

Instead of entering a keyword in the Hints box, put the title of the clip in quotation marks so that you get exactly the video you want.

Save your changes and make sure it works by looking at your Web page.

Sound like effort? It is a bit, and it would be nice to see Google make it all easier. Personally, I've found that making your own videos is a lot more fun...

I think these video units can be a great way to enhance the content on any website. They offer additional revenue streams — and give you one less content post that you have to create yourself.

Much though will depend on the sort of creators available in your content field or the clips that Google decides to give you.

Test to see whether Revver or Google gives you the most revenue — I suspect that it will depend on the content of the video, so make a point of searching both for good clips — then get into the habit of offering films about once a week.

11.11 AdSense for Games

There is one type of content that I really love: games. I'm a huge game player. In fact, one of my first forays into online marketing was to partner with a game developer to bring players into his online arcade.

We ended up selling that site to Yahoo! where it became Yahoo! Games.

Today, I'm not sure that I would sell a successful gaming site because thanks to Google it is now possible to make real money by placing ads in online games.

In the past, developers either had to approach advertisers themselves for product placement — which was difficult — or place ads on the page, around the game, which delivered poor results.

Because a page with a game has few words, receiving contextualized ads is tricky. And getting people to click is even harder. Users of game sites aren't interested in information; they want to play so they ignore the ads and head straight for the entertainment.

You can't blame them for that.

Google though has come up with a solution. *It now helps game publishers to embed their ads into the games themselves.* The ads come in all sorts of forms — text, video, flash and image — and can pay on either a CPM or CPC basis. Rather than appearing as an irritating overlay — as they do on videos — they can be placed at strategic points in the game, such as between levels, after tasks or on start-up.

That can make them unmissable and very effective indeed.

On the whole, users don't mind looking at ads if it means that they can play for free. Unlike other forms of online content, games are sold online and users are prepared to pay for them.

They understand that looking at an ad is a small price to pay for a game that would otherwise cost money.

There are just a couple of challenges to overcome before you can start earning from ads in games though...

Fig. 11.6 One of the first advertisers on Google's game network was insurance company,
Esurance, which embedded a neat video ad into a word game.

The first is getting hold of the games.

If you're a wonder with Flash, then you should be able to have some fun developing your own. If you're not though, you'll have to partner with a developer.

The easiest way to do that would be to pay a programmer to create a game for you. Find a programmer on Elance or Scriptlance, tell them what sort of games you'd like and hire them to do the job.

You'll get exactly the game you want, and you'll own it.

But that will be expensive. Even a simple, playable game will cost several thousand dollars to develop and while good marketing should ensure that you make that money back — perhaps by selling a downloadable, ad-free version as well — you will need to have a pile of start-up cash available... and a willingness to risk it.

An alternative is to form a partnership. This is what I did when I saw SpringerSpan.com, a games site that had fantastic multiplayer games... and no gamers. I used my marketing skills to bring in players and grew the site together with the developer until it was big enough to sell.

You could do something similar. If you know of a website or a developer who has lots of good games but is still under the radar, drop the publisher a line and suggest a partnership. You'll agree to place the games on your site, recommend it to your users and bring in new players in return for sharing the advertising revenue in the same way that you might do when partnering with a writer.

The developer is supplying the game; you're supplying the audience; and the advertisers are supplying the revenue.

To make such a partnership work though, you will need to get over the other challenge.

Google is restricting the program to publishers who generate... 500,000 game plays per day and whose traffic is at least 80 percent US or UK-based.

That's right, 500,000 game plays!

But no one gets 500,000 game plays. Even World of Warcraft, one of my favorites, would struggle to get half a million people through the doors in 24 hours. A really good game on a popular games site might generate 20,000 or 30,000 game plays a day if it's lucky.

That's why it's no surprise that Google has indicated that it is willing to look at publishers who have fewer game plays. You can't join up directly from your AdSense center but you can submit an application at services. google.com/events/adsense_games.

That does still leave the average publisher with a dilemma though.

Few publishers know how to design even simple Flash games, just as few games developers know how to bring traffic into a website and monetize it. While a partnership between an established publisher and a struggling games developer looks like an ideal solution then, *neither will be able to make money from Google's embedded ads until the game is already on the site and generating plays*.

Before you approach a publisher, you'll need to make it clear that there's no guarantee that you'll be accepted into the program and that there will be a period when you'll be splitting revenues from AdSense units placed around the game. You'll also need to place text on that page to help AdSense produce targeted ads.

To make the contact, you could send the developer an email like this:

Dear [developer],

My name is [your name], and I'm the publisher of [your site]. I've been playing your game [name of game], and I have to tell you that I've loved every minute of it. It's a fantastic game, with great graphics and it's a huge amount of fun.

I noticed though there are often times when you have few players. My site brings in [number] users every day, and I know many of them would love to play your game.

As I'm sure you know, Google now has a program that allows developers to embed ads into their games. And as I'm sure you also know, you need to have a lot of players to earn from those ads.

Here's what I propose. With your permission, I'll place your game on one of my AdSense-optimized Web pages, and market it on your behalf to my users. By alternating your AdSense code with my AdSense code, you will be able to earn half the ad revenue that page generates.

In addition, once we can see that the game is generating sufficient plays, we can submit it to Google's AdSense for Games programs and, if it's accepted, share an even larger payout.

If that sounds reasonable to you, do drop me a line and we can discuss it in more detail.

Best,
[Your name]
[Your site]

That sounds like a lot of effort. It certainly requires a lot more work than writing the odd blog post, offering half your ad revenue to writers or looking for good videos on YouTube.

But if you like gaming, it could give you a profitable website in a field that you love.

It might take effort, but it won't feel like work.

11.12 Earning From Creative Commons Images

Something that will feel like work though is hard labor, the punishment that used to be doled out to criminals. You won't get a sentence like that, but there is a chance that you've been breaking the law.

I'm sure you didn't do it on purpose — most publishers don't.

But many publishers still do it anyway.

In fact, according to one survey, *90 percent of the images used on websites are stolen.*

That doesn't mean that the publisher has slipped into a gallery in the middle of the night, hung from a harness and swiped a picture off the wall. It means that they've done a search on Google Images or spotted a photo they liked on a blog, right clicked, saved the image and used it themselves.

It's easy, it's convenient… and it's wrong.

Those pictures belong to people. You can't use them without the creator's permission. Usually, if the image-maker notices that you've breached their copyright, they'll ask you to give them a link in return— that's easy enough to do.

They might also say some rude things and ask that you take the picture down. That's unpleasant and inconvenient, but easy enough to handle too. Apologize and take the picture down.

But if your site has a lot of users and is clearly making a lot of money, there's a good chance that the photographer will go a little further and ask for compensation. Worse, if he's registered the image with the Copyright Office, he could ask for punitive damages too.

That could all get very expensive.

Fortunately, there are a couple of solutions and one of them is very useful indeed.

Microstock sites like iStock.com (www.istock.com) and Fotolia.com (www.fotolia.com) sell stock images for as little as a dollar apiece. They have millions of images to choose from, they're very high quality and at those sorts of prices there's really no need to steal images to decorate your website.

But there's also an option that's completely free.

Creative Commons licenses allow anyone to make use of artworks without paying a fee. They can be applied to anything, from articles to images and everything in between.

For publishers, they can be a very useful source of free content, especially for images.

There's a whole bunch of different Creative Commons (CC) licenses that let you do different things. You want to make sure that you choose a non-commercial license.

That means you're not expected to pay. Often though, the creator will demand attribution, which means you have to link back to the source of the image.

That's a pretty small price to pay.

Especially when you consider that you could create an entire blog based on CC-licensed images.

Flickr, for example, has over 70 million CC-licensed photos that anyone can take and place on their own websites for nothing!

To find them, you just have to conduct an "advanced search" at Flickr, enter your search term and make sure that you click the boxes marked "Only search within Creative Commons-licensed content" and "Find content to use commercially."

(Whether placing an image on an ad-supported website would be considered commercial use is debatable... but you want to make money not hold a debate with a photographer.)

Once you've found an image you like, you might even be able to choose the size you'd like to use on your site.

Fig. 11.7 Flickr lets you help yourself to more than 70 million free images. But make sure you only search among CC-licensed images. Flickr's photographers can be very protective of their images.

Of course, not all of those 70 million-odd images are going to be interesting. Many of them will be of birthday parties and Mexican vacations. But many of them will also be beautiful works of art shot by talented enthusiasts who get a kick out off showing off their work.

In addition to using Flickr as a source of free illustrations for your content then, one option then could be to create a site dedicated to a particular type of photography, such as car images, mountains or surf photography. Place new photos on the site every few days and put your AdSense code nearby.

You'll need a paragraph or two of text to go with each image — remember, Google's crawlers can't read pictures — and you should title the images and include ALT tags to help the crawler understand what's on your page.

But an approach like that could give you a huge and growing inventory of free content to use on your sites.

11.13 AdSense For Domains

And finally, here's something that goes against all of the principles of profitable online publishing...

It is now possible to make money from AdSense on websites that have absolutely no content at all.

That doesn't mean you can put up a blank page, paste in your AdSense code and wait for the check. Any check you do receive would be as empty as your content.

But you can put AdSense units and AdSense for Search on pages that are waiting to be developed.

Earning from parked sites has always been one strategy that Internet publishers have used to make money. Many publishers own hundreds, if not thousands, of domains and have only built on a handful of them. Some they plan to develop in the future, others could be used to block competing publishers, and many were bought as an investment to be sold at a later date.

There's little point in marketing pages like these. They don't have content, so Google won't index them and users won't come back to them, but some of these domains do receive traffic.

That traffic could come from people typing — or often, mis-typing — a URL directly into a browser, and it can also come from links to an extinct site that used to exist at that domain.

Hosting services allow publishers to park their sites and place ads on them in return for a large share of the revenue but now Google is getting in on the action by placing its own units on unbuilt pages.

For publishers, this can be a bonanza... but only a small one.

The terms for AdSense for Domains state specifically that publishers are not allowed to use online advertising to bring in traffic. In other words, you're only going to be earning from the natural traffic the domain receives.

But the amount you earn is likely to be higher than usual.

Users who reach an empty domain haven't found what they're looking for so they're keen to move on quickly. Because Google's units are always well-targeted to the subject of the domain or the keywords entered in the search box, the ads are likely to be clicked.

In fact, publishers have found that conversion rates on AdSense for Domain can be twice that of the ad units on their content pages!

To place AdSense on domains that you've bought but haven't yet built, you'll need to hit the AdSense Setup tab in your Google account, choose AdSense for Domains and agree to the terms and conditions. You'll then be able to enter your domain names. If you have a lot of them — and this is really the only way to make a decent amount of money with parked domains — then you can upload a CSV list containing as many as 1,500 domains.

The next step is a little tricky. You have to make some changes to your domain registrar's settings. This is a bit technical but Google does offer step-by-step guides to all of the main domain registration companies.

Follow the appropriate guide exactly and you should be fine.

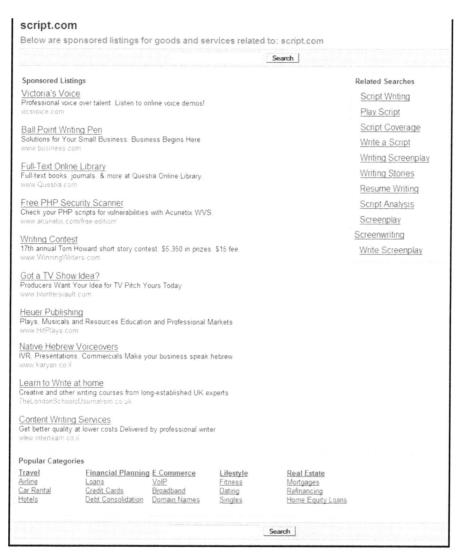

Fig. 11.8 AdSense for Domains lets you earn money from Google's ads even when you don't have content. This site though first showed links for programming scripts and then for screenplays.

You can also add channels so that you can track the results of each of your domains and play with your domain's color scheme.

This is actually one of the few factors that give you some control over the clickthrough rate. Ideally, you want to make the page look like content rather than an unbuilt domain. So you could try changing the background colors as well as the URL color. But you also need make sure that the links looks like links, that the text is easily read and the search field easy to find.

Try testing the standard white page, black text and blue links for a few weeks to give yourself a baseline, then test a different color scheme — keeping the links blue — to see which gives you the best results.

More important is the ability to add keyword hints.

Google only uses your domain name to decide which kinds of ads to serve so you really should be tossing in targeted keywords here. You want to make sure that people who reach your domain get to see ads for services that could interest them.

Even after you've come up with the best possible color scheme and included good keyword suggestions though, you can still expect to receive little more than a few cents a day. Multiplied over a thousand sites, that can be a useful extra income though and it may mean that if you decide to sell the domain, you'll be able to point to its current revenues when negotiating the price.

On the other hand, you're not allowed to put anything on the domain other than AdSense so you won't be able to indicate that the domain is available for sale.

That's something you'll need to consider too.

On the whole though, if you have any unbuilt domains and you're not thinking of selling them, placing AdSense units on them is a good way to earn a little extra income until you start developing.

12. DELIVERING CONTENT — ADSENSE BEYOND WEBSITES!

AdSense might originally have been designed to monetize websites but as digital content has expanded beyond sites themselves, so Google has found ways to place its ads everywhere... even in your pocket!

As you're building your Internet business, don't forget to look at additional ways to deliver your content. The more methods you can use to put your words — and ads — in front of readers, the more you can earn.

12.1 AdSense In RSS Feeds

One of the biggest changes to take place on the Internet recently has been the growth of RSS (Really Simple Syndication) feeds. These let users ask for new content to be sent to them directly instead of forcing them to visit a Web page to see it.

Subscribers can then open up a special RSS reader that lets them see the content that they've ordered.

It's a bit like receiving all the Internet you want by email.

For a long time, RSS was a bit of a dilemma for Internet publishers.

On the one hand, lots of people like to use it to read content, so not offering them RSS meant that they might not come back. Being able to see exactly how many subscribers you have also makes measuring one aspect of a site's performance very easy.

Even if subscribers represent only a fraction of your total users, they are likely to be your most dedicated readers and the rate at which the numbers rise and fall is a pretty good indication of how well you're appealing to your subject's core audience.

On the other hand, people who do receive content by RSS wouldn't be seeing your AdSense units. Although Yahoo!'s Publisher Network and Kanoodle, another advertising system, have long allowed ads in RSS feeds, neither produce the sort of results that can compete with Google's units.

In effect, RSS made it easier for your most dedicated users to enjoy your content... but it also made it harder for you to monetize them.

That's all changed.

After much experimenting and an invitation-only Beta program that took far too long to be expanded, Google now allows anyone to put AdSense units in their RSS feeds.

That makes it a must-have for just about every publisher who updates their content.

If you're using a blogging service like Blogger or Wordpress then adding an RSS feed to your site is just a matter of hitting the right link. Blogger, for example, has a link marked "Site Feed" under the Settings tab that brings up all of the options you need to set up your RSS.

The first option is the most important. It determines whether you send all of the article to the RSS reader or just the first paragraph or so.

One the one hand, readers will often unsubscribe if they can't see the whole article. You might be better off then giving them the whole article and inviting them back to your site to add and see comments.

On the other hand, clickthrough rates on feeds tend to be much lower than those on websites. If your users want to read all of your content, they should be willing to see ads and that means finishing their reading on your Web pages.

It might not be what your subscribers really want but it will still allow them to see what you've uploaded to your site, let you send them an ad, and bring them back to your site to read more... and serve them even more ads.

Test both options and see which works best for you.

Fig. 12.1 Google's Blogger makes creating RSS feeds really simple.
Other services are just as easy.

You'll want to make sure that your headlines are attractive and inviting. Many users don't look past them, so if they don't do the job, the post won't be opened or read, and the user won't click to your site. Images can also help your feeds to stand out.

It's rarely a good idea to send more than one RSS post to a subscriber each day. The most common reason that users unsubscribe isn't poor content or too much advertising, but too many posts.

One good strategy then is to divide your RSS feeds by theme and let subscribers only receive posts on the topics that interest them most. If you're writing about a range of different subjects, that should already help to keep the deliveries down to a manageable level.

Once you've set up a feed on your site, it's a good idea to sign up for Feedburner.

Feedburner is an RSS management system that is now owned by Google. It's free to use and, most importantly, it gives you all sorts of valuable statistics about your feed.

You'll be able to see the number of subscribers, the number of people who click through to your site and the popularity of particular articles. For anyone who reads their stats — and that should be every publisher who wants to make money from their website — that's all fascinating and useful stuff.

Signing up for Feedburner won't take more than a few minutes. You can even do it when you're signing up for AdSense for Feeds.

To place the ads, click the AdSense Setup tab in your AdSense account then choose AdSense for Feeds, and start creating your ad units.

Most of the options here are very straightforward. While you should test all of the options to see which work best for your readers, in general, you should:

- Choose to receive both text and image ads;
- Include ads in all your feed items;
- Place ads in posts of any length;
- Locate the ads at the bottom of the feed item.

Receiving both text and image ads will let Google figure out which are most likely to hand over the most money. Whenever you send out a feed, you want to make sure that you have some way of making money from it. And subscribers will look right past an ad at the top of a feed to read the content.

If they've been left hungry after they've finished reading though, there is a chance that they'll hit the ad.

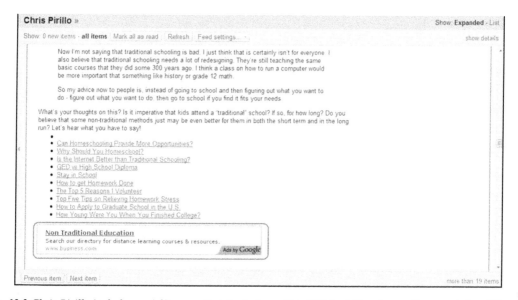

Fig. 12.2 Chris Pirillo includes an AdSense unit at the bottom of his RSS feed. Note how well targeted the ad is to the subject of the post... and how by placing a list of links at the bottom of his item, he helps to optimize the ad.

12. DELIVERING CONTENT — ADSENSE BEYOND WEBSITES! 111

The only option that might have you scratching your head is whether to allow AdSense to optimize the color choices automatically.

When it comes to optimization, I'm a bit of a control freak. Only if I've done everything myself can I feel certain that I'm making as much money as possible.

But different readers present feeds in different ways so manual optimization might give you great results in one reader, but not in another.

The best choice is to let AdSense optimize the ads at first to see what it comes up with... then do it yourself and see if you do any better.

AdSense on RSS feeds is very, very useful. Many users expect RSS feeds on blogs and not including one these days can cost you readers. But they're very difficult to monetize. Feed readers tend to be fairly sophisticated types who know exactly what they want and they can spot an ad at a hundred paces.

Google's move is a step in the right direction but don't expect your RSS feeds to deliver very high clickthroughs. The ads will help you to pick up a few more clicks, but the real money will come when the subscribers click through to your site and see the rest of your ads.

12.2 AdSense On Mobile Phones

RSS could prove to be a powerful revenue source for AdSense publishers. It can certainly be a good way to inform users that you've got new content and bring them back in to view it.

I'm not sure about AdSense on mobile phones.

AdSense started allowing publishers to place one ad unit on mobile Web pages in September 2007. You can select the colors, specify the kind of code your mobile page uses ("wml (WAP 1.x)", "xhtml (WAP 2.0)", or "chtml"), and choose ad units with images or one or two text-link ads (although the double unit can only appear at the bottom of the page.)

It sounds like a good idea, but AdSense for mobile has its challenges. For a long time, despite their promise, phones were good ways to surf the Web.

The screens were tiny, the downloads slow and it can be expensive. Most people are prepared to wait until they get home or to the office to look at a website, rather than do it on their mobiles.

There have long been exceptions. Surfing on phones has always been fairly popular outside America (especially in Japan). In the United States, it has often been used for information that changes quickly such as sports news or finance. If you had a site on either of those topics or which is popular in Asia, then you might have wanted to create a page that worked on a mobile, offer breaking news and place an ad on it to see how much it earns.

My feeling is that it wouldn't have been worth the effort and you would have been better off using your time to expand your site.

The situation is changing though. The iPhone, with its built-in wifi and big screen, has gone a long way towards changing the way people interact with the Web. Competitors have noticed the change and are also building mobiles with browsing in mind.

But the advantage of surfing on a large-screen mobile phone is that you can see the site as the publisher intended. You don't really need to create a special page design for the iPhone.

My feeling is that if you currently have a mobile website, AdSense for Mobiles might a pretty useful addition although you'd want to test it against AdMob, a rival service. Optimize the ads as much as you can and put them on the sort of content people on the move are likely to need.

But focus on building content for your site… and create apps for mobiles.

12.3 Use Your Newsletter To Drive Traffic!

So you can put your content in RSS feeds and you can broadcast it over mobiles.

You can also put your articles in newsletters and deliver them to email inboxes.

But you can't put AdSense ads in them. Google did test AdSense in newsletters with iVillage.com but it looks like they weren't happy with the results. The company states specifically that it "does not permit AdSense ad code to be placed in email messages or newsletters."

But that doesn't mean newsletters are useless though.

Newsletters are fantastic tools **to drive repeat visitors to your pages!**

Here's one way to use them: Instead of mailing the entire newsletter, save a few juicy tid-bits for your website and provide a link for your visitors to click.

When subscribers clickthrough to get the full story, they're likely to click your ads. And send you another AdSense bonanza! For example, Prizepot (www.prizepot.com), one of my sites, offers contests and sweepstakes with a new item each day. Our free weekly newsletter is sent with a teaser for all the new items posted that week. In order to find the entry form, you must click the link in the newsletter. Of course, when you arrive at the destination page, not only do you receive information about the contest, but you are greeted by AdSense ads. For a sample newsletter, send an email to join-prizepot@lists.worldvillage.com.

> If you have a big, responsive mailing list — start turning it now into extra AdSense cash!

You can either create a newsletter yourself — and mail it using a mass mailing system like Intellicontact. com — or you can ask someone to write it for you. ConstantConversions.com (www.constantconversions.com) is a copywriting service that specializes in newsletter writing. You can tell them about your site and they'll do it all for you, from concept to inbox. You can even tell them you want it optimized for AdSense. They'll know what to do.

 To start your own email newsletter and auto-responder for your site, I highly recommend Aweber.com. With Aweber, you can build unlimited lists with unlimited autoresponders. That means you can have your list set up to automatically send email to certain groups at predetermined times. Along with their email broadcast services, Aweber is my first choice for many of my lists.

Part
3

Following The Figures

13. HOW TO READ YOUR VISITORS LIKE A BOOK

13.1 Making Sense Of Stats, Logs And Reports...

Stats are a vital part of your success. If you can't follow the results of all the changes you're going to be making to your ads and your pages, then you're never going to maximize your revenues.

But reading your stats can be confusing. You're going to be staring at all sorts of tables filled with all kinds of numbers which can be rearranged and reorganized in all sorts of different ways.

That's why it's crucial to know how to read your stats and understand the figures.

13.2 The Most Important Stat Of All

There's one figure that's going to be more important than any of the others. Know which one I'm talking about?

Revenue! If you aren't making money, no other stats matter.

If you are making money though, the next stat you want to watch is your CTR. The higher the percentage of clicks to page impressions you receive, the higher your CPM will rise — and the higher your revenues will become.

When you make a change to your ad placement, to your keywords, to your ad colors or anything else, wait a week and check your stats to see the result. And look first at your revenues.

Bear in mind too that when you have multiple ads on a page each ad unit counts as one impression — but you won't be able to get three clicks from all of your units! Multiple ad units then can reduce your CTR while still giving you good revenues.

You might also want to translate your results into charts so that you can easily spot trends in CTR and in earnings. Tracking impressions will also let you see any radical fluctuations in traffic.

13.3 Optimum CTR

Much of your success will depend on lifting your CTR as high as possible. Obviously, the more people who click on your ads the more money you should make, and it is possible to improve your CTR. I've gone from a CTR of less than 1 percent to over 8 percent on some sites.

And I know of some sites that are getting CTRs of over 30 percent!

Your CTR will depend on a number of different factors, including:

- **Site Content** — Some types of content get more clicks than others (but don't necessarily make more money per click...)
- **Site Design** — We've already talked about the importance of where you place your ads and how you place them.
- **Number Of Links** — Why give your ads competition? If people want to click away from the page, you should get paid for it.
- **Ad Relevancy** — If you're not getting served ads that are relevant to your content, you're going to have a low CTR.

14. RESPONSE TRACKING: YOUR HIDDEN POT OF ADSENSE GOLD!

In Chapter 11, we talked about content. Google won't let you ask visitors to click on your ads, or use other deceptive ways to make them click. But good content is an endorsement in itself. Some of its charm rubs off on the ads, making the ads more believable — and interesting!

If you have a website with impartial product reviews, for instance, visitors are more likely to click the ads to learn more about a product, check out the latest prices or order online.

It's crucial to create content that's genuinely interesting. But your work doesn't stop there.

After setting up your AdSense Account, the first thing you want to do is play with your ad formats and placement to make the ads blend in. That's where the bulk of the "easy-money" is hiding.

But once you've got that right, what next? You start tweaking the text and making all sorts of other changes to improve your CTR.

But every time you make any sort of change to your ads, you must track the results.

This is a vital part of AdSense optimization and will make the difference between a small amount of money and earning the sort of amounts that AdSense can deliver.

Consider this example:

Joe Drinker has a great website about "How to make Beer at Home." It's doing well on AdSense, but not well enough. His week's stats look something like this:

Date	Page Impressions	Clicks	Page CTR	Page eCPM	Your earnings
3/2/09	40930	1516	3.7%	5.62	229.92
3/3/09	40358	1574	3.9%	6.59	265.99
3/4/09	38962	1517	3.9%	6.11	238.01
3/5/09	33563	1381	4.1%	6.38	214.21
3/6/09	32978	1325	4.0%	6.76	223.81
3/7/09	28207	1294	4.6%	7.52	212.01
3/8/09	27322	1251	4.6%	7.47	204.20

Joe is pretty happy with his CTR but wonders if he can raise his CPM and in the process, lift his earnings. So he looks up high-priced keywords related to his subject, and works the term "beer cans" into his content.

A few days later he logs into the stats on his AdSense account and finds that that change has actually HURT his income:

Date	Page Impressions	Clicks	Page CTR	Page eCPM	Your earnings
3/9/09	32744	985	3.0%	4.21	137.95
3/10/09	32286	1023	3.2%	4.94	159.59
3/11/09	30954	986	3.2%	4.59	142.08
3/12/09	26850	898	3.3%	4.78	128.52
3/13/09	26382	861	3.3%	5.08	134.28
3/14/09	22566	841	3.7%	5.63	127.20
3/15/09	21858	813	3.7%	5.60	122.52

Joe has not only disappointed a lot of collectors who come looking for beer cans — his site contains lots of keywords but little in the way of good content — he has also discouraged visits from people who want to make beer at home.

His search ranking has gone down, making his website harder for people to find him and lowering his impressions. It's also hurt his earnings per click as the people who visit the site leave faster. What's worse is that he's also risked his AdSense standing!

Now, does that make it a bad idea to optimize your website for AdSense?

Not at all. It is actually a good idea, if you do it right. And by that I mean… No Shortcuts!

There is a simple, step-by-step process to optimize your website for high-paying search terms. And this method is almost fool-proof! So why isn't everybody doing this?

Simply because very few web publishers know how to use Tracking to their advantage.

Tracking will not only help you minimize your mistakes, it will also reveal hidden pockets of money that you would have never found otherwise.

Read on to find out how YOU can use Tracking to sky-rocket your CTRs and increase revenues per-click.

14.1 How To Track With Channels

Google has its own FREE tracking feature called "Channels." Channels remind me of spy movies, where a smart chip is planted in the arm of a super sleuth, making it easier to track his activities or whereabouts.

AdSense now hands you 200 such chips. Use them to track ads on specific domain names or to group ads according to specific ad formats, keywords, their location on the page, etc. You can use any other factor that might impact their effectiveness, based on the type of website you have.

Channel those clicks!

Google tells you many things about each channel, such as the ad impressions, clickthroughs and earnings data.

You can use the channel reports to find out which channels are making you the most money — and how to increase your earnings for other channels.

14.2 How To Create A URL Channel

Google lets you create two kind of channels: URL channels and custom channels.

With **URL channels** you can track clicks across your site's pages. You can do this by entering four different kinds of URL in the "create new channel" box. Each type of channel gives you information of different accuracy:

example.com tracks all the pages in your site and gives a general picture of what your site is doing;

subdomain.example.com tracks all the pages in one particular subdomain;

subdomain.example.com/widgets tracks all the pages in a specific directory;

and **subdomain.example.com/page.html** tracks the clicks on one specific page.

That's a huge range of choices, from an overview of a site that might have hundreds of pages through groups of pages that concern particular subjects to the clicks you're getting on just one page.

So if you had three sites, one about custom cars, one about custom bikes and one about speedboats, the first thing you'd do is create a general channel for each site.

You should always create a channel for each one of your sites.

That will let you see not just how much money you're making overall, but how much money each site is making. You're not going to get too far without that sort of information!

Now, let's say that the custom car site had tabs for American cars, European cars, Japanese cars and classic cars. Each tab is a subdomain and you could create a channel for each subdomain too. Now you could see which topic is making the most money.

And if you discussed one car on each page, you could also create channels for the individual pages and see which cars are the most popular and deliver the highest earning clicks.

Sounds good, right?

And it's now very easy to do.

Back in the bad old days, Google required you to **manually change AdSense tags** for each ad block you wanted to track. Many AdSense partners complained about these pesky old channels until Google launched the URL channels to make life easier.

Now all you have to do is sign in and click the tab marked "AdSense Setup" followed by the "Channels" link.

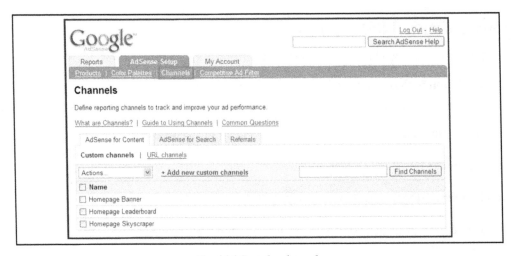

Fig. 14.1 Spot the channels

And the next step is to use the link marked "URL Channels" and enter the URLs you want to track.

That's it! You don't have to do anything else. Google will start tracking the URLs you've added automatically.

So apart from creating URL channels for each of your sites, which of the other URL channels should you create?

As far as I'm concerned, you can't have too much information. Major areas should certainly be covered and if you can go as far as tracking each page without going over the 200 channel limit, so much the better. It's certainly worth tracking a few individual pages to make sure that the revenues are spread out across different parts of the site.

If you find that one page is making lots of money and another is making none, you'll want to know the reason why.

14.3 How To Create A Custom Channel

The URL channels are especially useful if you have several websites, and have a general idea of the formats, colors, alignment etc. that works best for you.

Remember though, you still need the original, **Custom Channels** if you want to track ads across different domain names based on ad sizes, formats, colors, etc.

For instance, if I want to track left-aligned ads across all my websites (sites with different domain names), I need to group them together into a single channel and change the channel code for each page.

First, I name the new channel:

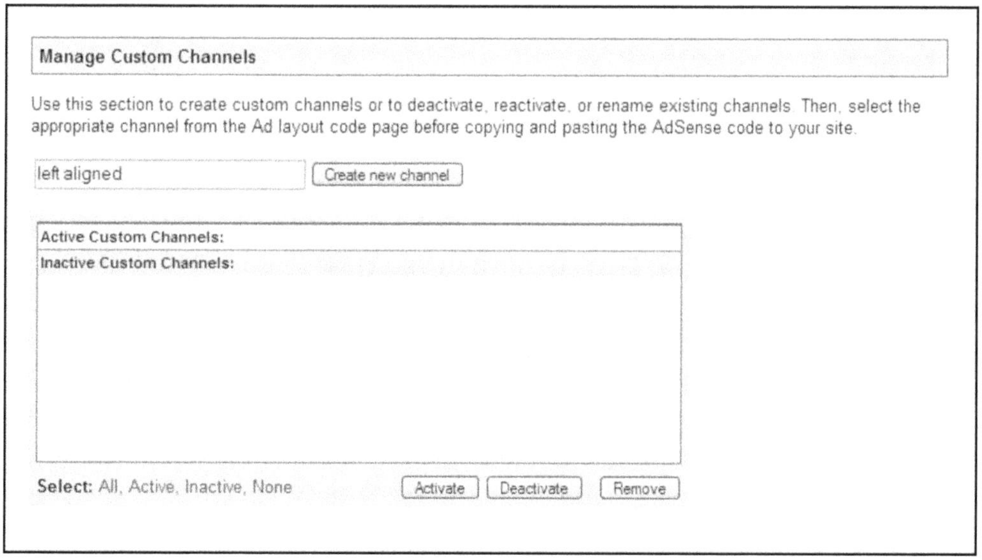

Fig. 14.2 Here comes a new channel...

Then I choose the Ad Type, Layout and Color of the ads I want to track:

Finally, it's simply a matter of allocating an alternate URL if I don't want public service ads, selecting the channel and copying **and pasting the code onto each of the pages that contain these kinds of ad**.

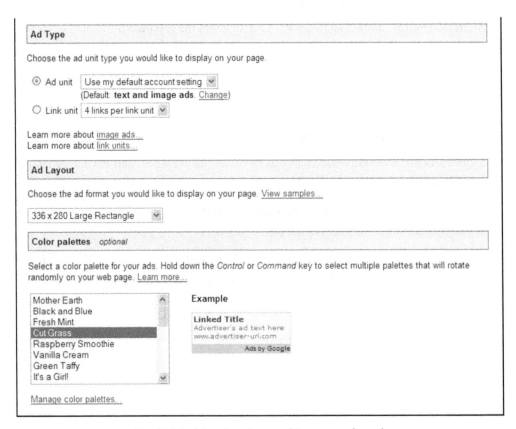

Fig. 14.3 Defining the ads to track in my new channel.

Of course, I would then have to repeat the process if I wanted to track ads of a particular color or size.

That's very different to the process you use to create a URL channel.

URL channels are tracked automatically without the need for you to paste code. With custom channels, you're going to have to go back to your own site, add the code in the appropriate pages and upload the changes to your server.

While that's a bit of a headache, it's a headache worth having.

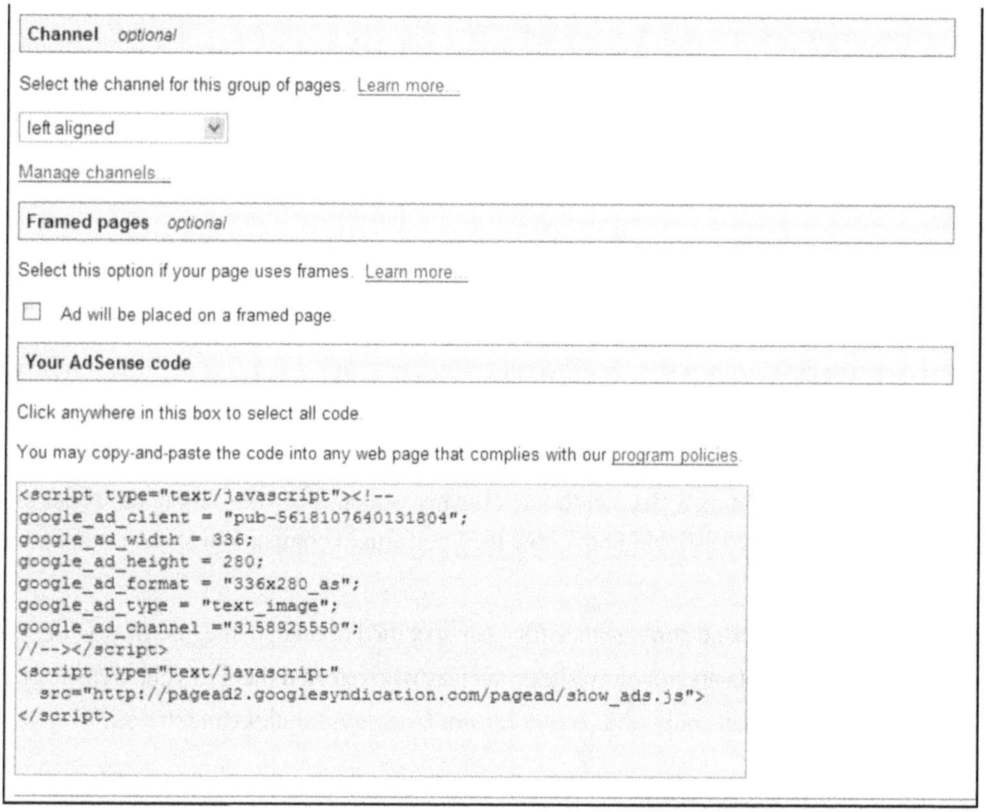

Fig. 14.4 Creating the code for my new channel.

Custom channels provide such a broad range of information — from how different locations are doing to how particular types of ad units affect your revenues — that without them, you're working in the dark.

14.4 What Custom Channels Should You Create?

With the range of custom channels limited only by your imagination, it's not always easy to figure out which channels you need to create.

I'd recommend that you build channels based on the following:

Location

Do ads do better at the top of your blog pages or on the side? Do you get more clicks from ads that you've slipped into the article or from the ads at the bottom of the page.

Try creating different channels for each sort of location so that you can track how different locations are doing.

Ad Unit

Different ad units can deliver different results. You might be using four or five different types of ad units across your sites. Make a channel for each type of unit so that you can get an idea about which units are the most attractive.Of course, location and ad unit are related but you won't be able to untangle the data unless you have it!

Color

I keep saying that the color of your ads should match the color of your site. But not all your sites are the same color! You might well find that some color schemes win you more clicks than others — a fact which could influence your overall site design.
Create different custom channels for different colors and you'll have a better idea of how your designs affect your income.

Link Units

It's certainly worth creating a channel to track the performance of your link units. These are special in their own right and you should know how they perform in comparison to your other ad units.

While Google can now track ad performance for your specified domain name, please don't expect URL or custom channels to give you data about your visitors, such as who referred them to your website or which web browser they use. These are details only your server logs or Google Analytics can tell you.

14.5 Creating Multiple Channels

In the past, one of the biggest challenges for publishers was to decide which characteristic they should track on each of their ad units. Should they follow an ad unit's color? Its position? Its size?

Now those decisions are much easier.

It's possible to paste up to five channel codes into one ad unit, allowing publishers to collect different information about the same ad. When you check your channels, you'll be able to how all your leaderboards or doing, as well as all your ads related by topic or color.

That's a huge help when it comes to understanding what your site is doing.

14.6 Your Channel Names — How To Keep Your Channels Secret And Win Channel Targeted Ads

Channels are extremely useful tools. You won't be able to make the most of your site unless you're using channels to track the performance of your ad units — and acting on what you find.

But there is one small problem with using channels: the channel name appears in your source code.

That's unlikely to cause you any serious problems but it is something you need to know. There are two reasons for that.

First, you always want to maintain your privacy and create a professional impression. If you're making your site available to the public — which is the only way it's going to make money — you don't want anything on there that you wouldn't want the world to know. That includes the terms you've used for your custom channels.

But the second reason is that when you create your channels, you'll also be asked to mark a checkbox that says: "Show this channel to advertisers as an ad placement." If you mark that box — and you should — **advertisers will be able to try to place their ads across that channel.** (They'll still have to bid in the usual way but if the advertisers are keen enough to choose your site by channel, there's a good chance that they'll also be keen enough to bid high enough to win.)

So if you've created a channel for all of the ad units placed at the top of your Web pages, then an advertiser who chose to advertise across that channel could be sure that his ads would get prime placement.

That mean your channel names should be clear not just to yourself but to anyone else looking in too. If a channel that tracks the ad units embedded in articles about Toyota cars for example, is called "Toy_art," an advertiser could get the wrong idea... if he has any idea at all. If the channel were called "Toyota_articles" though, he'd know exactly where his ads would appear.

But getting the name right isn't the only thing you should do to tempt advertisers to bid on channel-targeted ad placements. You should also **add a description that makes it both clear to advertisers what exactly they'll be getting when they bid and attractive for them to do so**. Something like: "Ads will appear in our top-performing units: above the fold and embedded in our main article."

In fact, Google recommends that you use 300x250 medium rectangles embedded into text and available for both image and text ads for ad targeting. These, the company says, are the types of ads most in demand by advertisers.

That should help to encourage users to place your ads.

And once you've come up with a good channel name, don't change it. If an advertiser has picked your channel to place one of his ads and you change its name, you'll lose that advertiser.

14.7 Pick Up Separate Stats For Link Units

Many publishers used to create a specialized channel to track the results of their link units.

That's still a good idea. In fact, a change to the way AdSense reports on link units means that keeping a close eye on how those units are doing is now even more important than ever.

Select the Choose Units option in the Advanced Reports page and you'll be able to look at Ad Units, Link Units or both combined. Look at the Link Units and you'll be able to see the CTR of each link and the number of clickthroughs on the ads that the link generates. (Remember, link units lead to an ad page, not the advertiser's home page. Users have to click twice for you to get paid.)

That can give you some pretty interesting information.

It's always been believed the CTR of the ad page is much, much higher than the CTR of the link units themselves. Now we can see that's true. It's not unusual, for example, for the ad page to have a CTR as high as 7 percent — much higher than the links themselves.

What we can't do though is take action to improve the ad page CTR. We can't change the layout of the ad page or optimize it in any way to make it more attractive to users.

That means that only one factor will determine whether lots of people click the ads, or whether they click away.

The ads themselves.

Now, you can't choose the ads either but what you can do is create channels for different link units on different keyword-optimized Web pages. You'll then be able to see which keywords have the best ads and the highest clickthrough rates.

Most importantly, you'll be able to see whether it's worth replacing those link units with other ad units, or targeting different keywords on the page using AdSense's Section Targeting.

14.8 How To Read Your Server Logs

Various AdSense Tracking programs are currently sold on the Internet. This type of software runs on your own server which means it has access to vital visitor information.

These packages are not affiliated with Google, but you can use most of them without violating the AdSense TOS.

External tracking software can tell you many things that the channels don't reveal, such as:

- Where your visitors are coming from;
- Where the ad-clickers are coming from;
- What search keywords led them to your web page.

Your stats package should compile and interpret your log files. It will tell you how many people visited your pages, how long they stayed, which are the most popular pages, what countries/domains they visit from, and how many bookmarked your site.

Just about all the information you need.

One thing that external Tracking software **cannot** do for you, is to tell you **exactly how much MONEY** a specific ad (or a group of ads) is making for you. Only Google's channels can tell you that.

External tracking software can tell you an ad's CTR, but your AdSense income also depends on factors such as the earnings per click, content relevance, your ranking on Google Search Results and many other factors besides.

> I do recommend the use of external tracking software in addition to Google's channels.

Why? Because channels can be quite confusing if you use them by themselves. Consider this example:

Jim has a website about fast cars where he discusses his passion with thousands of like-minded visitors. He decides to find out which ads are doing better than the others.

Jim groups all ads with a blue border into a specific channel, which he calls "Blue_Border". He finds that the blue-border ads generated a 5% CTR, while the rest of the ads generated around 2% CTR on average:

Channel	Ad Unit Impressions	Clicks	Ad Unit CTR	Ad Unit eCPM	Your earnings
Blue_border	11378	569	5.0%	7.24	82.38
Green_text	11205	525	2.0%	6.29	70.54
Tall ads	12963	302	2.3%	1.22	15.78

Next morning Jim tweaks all his ads to give them a blue border. The result? The ads in the "Blue_Border" channel continue to generate 5% CTR, while the rest of the ads (which also have a blue border now) are still generating 2% CTR. Very confusing!

Channel	Ad Unit Impressions	Clicks	Ad Unit CTR	Ad Unit eCPM	Your earnings
Blue_border	11606	590	5.0%	7.24	86.50
Green_text	11765	55	2.0%	6.29	74.07
Tall ads	12315	287	2.3%	1.22	14.99

Clearly, there's something else that's making Jim's visitors click — and it probably has nothing to do with the blue border.

14. RESPONSE TRACKING: YOUR HIDDEN POT OF ADSENSE GOLD!   129

What is that hidden ingredient that's jacking up those click-through ratios? The channels won't tell.

Jim now decides to install external tracking software on his website. After looking through his server logs, he finds that ads with the term "Car Accessories" are getting the maximum clickthroughs. How does Jim know that?

Simple. His tracking software tells him which ads his visitors are clicking. He also knows which sites his visitors are going to.

Jim found that of all his visitors, those who searched for the term "Car Accessories" were generating the maximum clickthroughs on his web pages. Naturally, ads with the term "Car Accessories" were doing better than the others.

Should Jim now optimize his website for the search term "Car Accessories"?

For most web publishers, that's good enough to get down to work.

But Jim is skeptical. **Jim wants to know if his "Car Accessories" ads are also his top income generators.**

To find out, he creates a channel to track the earnings of all ads with the term "Car Accessories" in it. He calls the new channel "Car_Accessories".

A few days later, Jim logs in to his AdSense account to check his earnings. He finds that about 30% of his income is drawn from visitors looking for car accessories.

Channel	Ad Unit Impressions	Clicks	Ad Unit CTR	Ad Unit eCPM	Your earnings
Car Accessories	14577	729	5.0%	4.9	71.43

That's significant, but it raises another question in Jim's mind.

Where is the remaining 70% of his income coming from?

He looks through his tracking reports once again and finds that ads with the term "Car Parts" are also doing well. He found that while "Car Accessories" took the lead with 5% CTR, the "Car Parts" ads were generating a healthy 3% CTR.

Jim is excited. He knows he's on to something big!

Jim's tracking software has helped him uncover two great "leads." Which of these will lead him to his top income generator?

The plot thickens…

To find out, Jim now creates another channel called "Car_Parts."

A week later, he logs in to compare his earnings for each channel.

Here are Jim's results:

Total AdSense income for one week = $1666.67

"Car_Accessories" Channel = $500 (30% of total AdSense earnings)

"Car_Parts" Channel = $1000 (60% of total AdSense earnings)

Remaining Ads = $166.67 (10% of total AdSense earnings)

Incredible! Jim now knows that his "Car_Accessories" ads might be getting him the most clicks, but **his "Car_Parts" ads are making him the most money!**

Google won't tell you all reasons why the "Car_Parts" ads are making Jim more money. But Jim knows that the keyword "Car Parts" is probably more expensive, and that his website ranks better for that term.

FINALLY--

Jim is ready to act on this information. Let's take a look at his various options:

1. He can use it to optimize his page for the search term "Car Parts" so that his content is more relevant. Jim knows from experience that when his ranking for the search term "Car Parts" goes up, so will his earnings per click.

   But it does have a downside. It might LOSE him his "Car Accessories" traffic! Jim knows that the price of keywords keeps fluctuating with the bids placed by AdSense advertisers. A keyword that's not so hot today can trigger a frenzied bidding war tomorrow!

   Jim doesn't want to lose his most responsive visitors, earning him a decent $500 per week.

2. Jim can optimize his page for "Car Accessories." But that comes with the huge risk of losing a whopping 60% of his earnings.

3. Jim can launch dedicated web pages for "Car Parts" and "Car Accessories."

4. Jim can optimize his page for BOTH search terms.

Jim decides to go with option 4 — optimize for BOTH search terms! Jim knows the old saying that if you try to please everyone, you end up pleasing no one at all. That's why he decides to play his cards carefully.

Jim understands visitor behavior. He knows that his visitors like to read in "bite sized" portions. They take a bite here and a nibble there. But they never read a web page like a book, starting from the top and reading right through to the bottom.

14. RESPONSE TRACKING: YOUR HIDDEN POT OF ADSENSE GOLD! 131

He tweaks his layout to make the "Car Parts" articles more visible. He smartly uses the hot car photos on his website to create several points of interest in his neatly laid out website.

Jim knows that people will instinctively look at the car photos, then be drawn in by detailed information about car parts — followed by the strategically placed Google ads.

To leverage this opportunity, Jim creates new space for content by tweaking the framework of his web page. Now Jim can capitalize his page layout by drawing people in with short, interesting 'content hooks' that build interest in the Google ads.

He adds new side-bars with juicy tidbits about hot new car accessories. These will act like instant magnets to visitors looking for car accessories. More importantly, they run right alongside the AdSense ads which tempt people with hot new offers on Car Accessories.

A specially designed "Accessories I love" section invites visitors to scroll down for more. Here Jim provides news, updates and impartial reviews about the Car Accessories Market. He entices visitors to check out new product launches with an integrated Google search box, which enables them to search within his website or search the entire web for relevant content.

These changes not only make Jim's Web pages more relevant; it makes his visitors more receptive to the ads. And there's more. Jim can now create new income streams for himself by plugging in new links to pages dedicated to car accessories, car parts and other keywords that are already attracting highly responsive visitors to his existing pages.

Jim used his channels and server logs to drill deep and come up with a real gold-mine of information. You too can use these secrets to **zero in on ads that make you the most money** — and to find hidden sources of AdSense income.

14.9 Fast Decision-Making With A/B Testing

One of the problems with tracking channels is that collecting all the data you need can take time. If you wanted to know whether you should put a skyscraper or a small square in your sidebar, you'd have to start with one type of ad unit, collect results for at least a week to make sure that they're representative, replace that unit with the second type, follow those results for a week and compare.

Sound tough?

Well, now there's an easier way.

Normally, playing with the AdSense code is a big no-no. But this script comes right from Google itself and has been approved for this specific use only:

```
<script type="text/javascript">
   var random_number = Math.random();
   if (random_number < .5){
      //your first ad unit code goes here
   } else {
      //your second ad unit code goes here
   }
</script>
<script type="text/javascript"
src="http://pagead2.googlesyndication.com/pagead/show_ads.js"></script>
```

Simply, replace the lines that say "your first ad unit code goes here" and "your second ad unit code goes here" with the ad codes for each of the two units you wish to test.

The result will be that the two ads are rotated randomly so that each will appear half the time. **As long as those two ad units are similar in every respect but one <u>and each has a unique channel name</u>**, you'll be able to see exactly which type of ad unit is earning more after about a week or so.

This is an extremely useful exception to AdSense's rules about changing its ad code, but I wouldn't recommend that you do it across your entire site. It's always best to do your testing on a separate page or group of pages and then make the changes across the site once you've got the information you want.

That would minimize your losses if the original ad unit works better.

14.10 The Easy Way To Make Changes!

So gathering the data you need is now easy. But what about acting on that information? If you find that B is better than A, you have to generate new code and go through your site replacing the old units with the new one.

If the ad unit only appears on one page, that's not a big deal. But if the same type of ad appears on hundreds of different pages, it's going to be a very big headache.

Or at least it used to be.

One of the changes that Google has made to AdSense since launching the service makes changing your code a great deal easier. The company's ad management feature lets you save the settings of your ads inside your AdSense account. When you then change the color or the channel name of a unit, the change will be made automatically wherever that unit appears. You won't have to copy and paste a thing.

Unfortunately, it doesn't apply to old units and you can't change the size of the units in this way.

But it's still a very neat trick and one that's going to save a huge amount of time.

When you create the ad unit, you will need to give it a name so that AdSense knows which unit to change, but that's no bad thing either. Often, you'll be able to use the channel name... which makes it less likely that you'll forget to create a channel for all your units and miss out on some valuable information.

And to make sure that you don't accidentally wipe out ad units that are earning you money, Google lets you "hide" them on your ad management page rather than delete them.

They know us too well...

14.11 Tracking Tools

There's a whole range of different tracking tools available to fill the gaps left by Google's channels. Here is a quick run-down of the main ones:

AdSense Log

www.metalgrass.com/adsenselog/index.html

Created by MetalGrass, this stats analyzer has easy-to-read graphs and charts. It also uses Google's own stats rather than tapping into your server's MySQL.

You can check your account as frequently as you want and the log will even you give you a sound, an email or a pop-up window when new data is available.

It costs $69.95 but is free until your earning reach $100 per month.

AsRep

www.asrep.com

AsRep lets you track all of your stats in real time. That includes each of your three regular ad units, an AdLink unit and up to two search boxes on each page.

The program also captures colors, format and channels, and whether the units are showing ads or alternates.

The price $50 but a free trial version is available.

CSV AdStats

www.nix.fr/en/csvadstats.aspx

CSVAdStats

CSV AdStats is less of a tracker and more of a number-cruncher. You can download Google's CSV data file and conduct a full stats analysis to check averages and create charts.

A useful way to squeeze more sense out of your stats and it's free!

14.12 Making Sense Of Google Analytics

Following your stats is vital. But I can't tell you that it's fun. Making money with AdSense is a business and like any business, it requires crunching numbers and making sense of figures.

It's not simple and it's rarely enjoyable. But you have to do it.

Google, helpful as always, has come up with a program that tries to make things a little easier.

Google Analytics is a completely free stats service that provides a ton of useful data about your website. You can sign up at www.google.com/analytics/. Then it's just a matter of pasting a few lines of code — like your AdSense code — onto each page of your website.

The result will be a phenomenal amount of information.

You'll see a graph showing your page views, bounce rate, number of unique visitors and average time on site.

You can see your traffic sources and the keywords people used to reach your site, review which pages are most popular and even set goals such as leaving an email address or making a purchase to see what percentage of users complete them.

That's all hugely valuable stuff… and it's likely to be the sort of thing that you can get from your server logs too.

But not only is Google Analytics easier on the eyes than most server logs, it's also integrated with Google's other services.

So in addition to being able to see the usual stats on your website, you'll also be able to see the results of any AdWords campaign that you're running… and now you can see some AdSense information too.

Link your Google Analytics account with your AdSense account, and you'll get ten additional pieces of information: total AdSense revenue; AdSense revenue per 1,000 visits; number of AdSense ads clicked; number of AdSense ads clicked per visit; clickthrough rate; AdSense eCPM; AdSense unit impressions served; AdSense unit impressions served per visit; AdSense page impressions served; and AdSense page impressions served per visit.

Sound complicated?

It shouldn't do. Most of those categories are pretty self-explanatory. And few of them are relevant.

What is complicated in fact, is figuring out which information is unnecessary, which is important... and what's been left out.

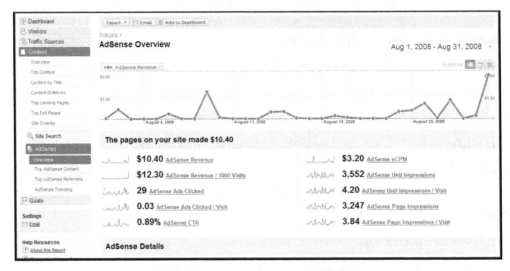

Fig. 14.7 Google Analytics provides ten different AdSense metrics but what do you really need to know?

Clearly, your **total revenues** are going to be vital and having your **clickthrough rate** right in front of you should make life much easier than having to work it out.

Google Analytics then lets you break down your revenues by time and location. So you can see which days — and even which hours — yielded the most money and which cities your users are in.

Neither of that information is going to be too helpful.

If your site has content with local interest then maybe seeing which areas you're missing could have a use but otherwise there's little point in trying to target your user base geographically. In general, users from the US, Canada and Western Europe tend to deliver higher prices from advertisers but if you're writing in English, you can expect most of your readers to come from the US anyway.

It's unlikely to matter where in the US they're from.

Similarly, traffic flows on the Internet are like traffic flows on the road. Some days there's a lot of it and some days there's none. On the Web, it's even worse than that: some hours, there's a lot of it and other times, there's practically no one on the site. And no one ever knows why.

There are a couple of tables on Google's Analytic's AdSense statistics that are very interesting though.

The first shows the **highest earning content pages**. That's fascinating stuff. Right away, you can see which pages — and which topics — are generating the most clickthroughs and the highest revenues.

In theory then, that table should tell you which subjects really interest your readers the most. If you can see, for example, that three of your five highest-earning revenue pages are about home-brewed beer then you might feel you should be writing more articles about home-brewed beer.

In practice though, you'll need to do a little more digging before you can come to firm conclusions.

Before you do anything, you'll want to make sure that it's only the topic that's making the difference between the pages and not the ad placements or the unit optimizations. So compare those high-earning with lower-earning pages first to see what else could be affecting clickthroughs and revenues.

If a lower earning page has different ad optimization, then change the ads before you start producing more of the high-earning content and test the results.

The second table is a little clearer. This shows your most important **referrers**.

Again, this is something your server logs should be able to tell you but it's useful to have all of the information in one place and it means you can target your content to suit traffic coming from specific sites.

So if you can see that much of the traffic to your site about entertaining is coming from a site about home-brewing, then that might explain why the pages about home-brewed beer receive the most clickthroughs... and what you should be writing about in the future.

But there's lots more information that Google could have supplied and didn't.

Google Analytics won't tell you, for example, *which ads* received the most clicks. Nor will it tell you which ad units or where those ad units are located.

Google Analytics then is a trove of useful information. But you will still need to create channels to cover metrics such as location, keywording, color schemes and formatting to know how all of the different optimization strategies affect revenues.

When you've created channels for all of the different metrics on your site, you should find that Google Analytics gives you a good overall picture of traffic flows and user behavior to and from your website... while the channels give you specific information about which ads are most likely to generate clicks.

To use Google Analytics, you should be able to simply click a link under the Advanced Reports link under Reports.

Google hasn't rolled the system out to everyone yet but if you don't see the invitation you should be able to find an application for an invitation at spreadsheets.google.com/viewform?key=pD9DqwPQLWy_ y9v1JWdDFSQ. Fill that out and the invitation should come through in about two days.

14.13 AdSense Arbitrage

Once you get to grips with the numbers that you see on the stats pages and your logs, you might notice something interesting. You might see for example, that you're getting 5,000 ad clicks on a page each month and that that page is generating $1500.

Divide $1500 into 5,000 clicks and you'll realize that each click for that type of content is bringing you 30 cents.

That means that when you come to buy content, as long as you spend less than 30 cents for a click to that page, you're going to make a profit. And one way to do that is to open an AdWords account and buy advertising space on Google's search pages. You could pay as little as 5 cents per click, giving you a profit of 25 cents each time your 5-cent users click on your 30-cent ads.

That's AdSense arbitrage and it sounds like a foolproof way to increase your revenues.

If it were that easy, everyone would be doing it.

The first problem with arbitrage is that you can never get a 100 percent CTR. Not every 5 cent click you buy is going to give you 30 cents back — and every impression that doesn't result in an ad click is going to eat into your profits.

With these kinds of figures (and obviously, yours are going to be different), you'd need a 16 percent CTR to break even. (If every ad click costs 5 cents and gives you 30 cents, you can afford to lose five out of every six clicks or 16 percent).

So if you can see that you're getting a 16 percent CTR, buying advertising on AdWords to send traffic to your AdSense ads could be a good deal.

Or not.

The second problem with arbitrage is that your CTR rate is based on users coming from your current traffic sources. The users you buy through AdWords might behave differently. They've already clicked on an ad once so they might not want to click on an ad again.

Or alternatively, because you know they're the type who do click on ads, it's possible that they're exactly the type who'll click on the ads on your page.

Results from using arbitrage vary. Some people report that the clicks they buy on AdWords give them less revenue, others report that they've increased their CTR.

The real key to arbitrage success is buying traffic based on the right keywords. And to do that you need...

14.14 WordTracker

WordTracker is a great way to find keywords to target for arbitrage. The idea is simple: if you can find popular keywords that few sites are targeting, you can increase the CTR of the ads you buy *and* improve the chances that users will click on the ads on your page. It's those keywords that will give you the best revenues for arbitrage — and the most clicks from search engine listings.

WordTracker actually helps in four different ways.

First, you enter a keyword — say, "football." WordTracker will then give you a list of *hundreds* of different keywords related to football — words like "stadium" and "team" and "football player." Some of those words you'll probably have thought of, but lots of them you won't.

Now you've already got more keyword options than when you started!

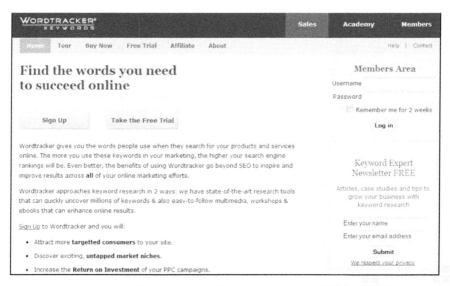

Fig. 14.9 WordTracker: "The best you need to succeed."

The next step is to see how popular these keywords are. WordTracker looks across all of the main search engines and tells you how many people searched for each keyword in the last 60 days. That's certainly interesting information in itself but there's not much point in targeting a word that 1,000 people search for every couple of months if a million Web pages are already targeting it.

Your ad would appear on page fifty-something of a search engine listing and get very few clicks.

The next stage is where things get really interesting. **Wordtracker compares the number of searches that people are making for each keyword with the number of sites targeting that keyword.**

It even awards each keyword a score that indicates the size of the opportunity for new pages that want to target that particular keyword. It then becomes easy for you to see which words are likely to give the best search engine listings — and which will get the most clicks for the lowest prices when you pay to advertise.

For example, if you asked WordTracker to look up the word "football," you might find that 3,474 people look for "shoulder-pads" each day but only 2,375 Web pages are targeting that word. If one of the pages of your football site targets that keyword, you're almost certainly going to find yourself high on the search engine listings, giving you plenty of free traffic.

But if you also choose to pay to advertise your site on Google, you can be confident that you'll get plenty of clicks — and great revenues.

WordTracker is a fantastic tool. It should definitely be in your money-making toolkit. Take a look at it at www.wordtracker.com.

15. SMART PRICING... AND WHAT IT MEANS FOR YOUR INCOME

One of the more difficult aspects of using AdSense is keeping up to date with changes that Google likes to introduce from time to time. Most of these changes are pretty minor. That doesn't mean that you can ignore them — you will need to be aware of them. But you won't usually have to make massive changes to your site and the way you've optimized your ads when Google adjusts its policy.

One change that did have a dramatic effect on publishers took place in April, 2004. Google introduced Smart Pricing. We've already felt some of its effects in this book. Now I'm going to explain exactly what it means...

First, let me just say that Smart Pricing *was* a pretty smart move, especially for advertisers. The principle is simple: before Smart Pricing, advertisers paid the price they had bid for each click their ad received on a website... regardless of whether that click resulted in a sale. The result was that some advertisers were receiving large numbers of clicks — for which they were paying large sums of money — but were seeing only a low return on that investment (ROI).

Not surprisingly, they were drifting away to other ad distributors, particularly Yahoo!, in the search for visitors who wouldn't just click but buy too.

To improve advertisers' ROI (and win them back from Yahoo!), Google lowered the price of ads on sites that tend to give advertisers few sales, even if they did give them large numbers of clicks.

The result is that the same ad can now cost different amounts when it appears on different sites. And of course, **that same ad will pay publishers different amounts too.**

Before Smart Pricing, publishers had focused solely on attracting as many clicks as possible. With Smart Pricing, a site with a high CTR can still earn *less* than a site with a low CTR.

So how does Google measure an advertiser's conversion rate and what can publishers do to increase their conversion rates to ensure their ad rates remain high?

This is where things get tricky. Google is playing its cards pretty close to its chest when it comes to the methods it uses to calculate Smart Pricing and even measure ROI.

15.1 What Google Has Said About Smart Pricing

This is what Google has officially told us about Smart Pricing:

- **The price of an ad is influenced by a number of different factors.**
  Those factors can include: the bid price; the quality of the ad; competition from other ads in the same field; the location of the ad as part of a marketing campaign; "and other advertiser fluctuations."

- **The ad price is <u>not</u> affected by the clickthrough rate.**
  Sending advertisers large numbers of clicks will *not* increase the bid price. (That doesn't mean that CTR isn't important at all for your revenues; it's just not important in determining the amount you receive for the click.)

- **"Content Is King."**
  Google makes it pretty clear that sites that will benefit most from AdSense are those that "create compelling content for interested users." They also emphasize the importance of bringing targeted traffic to look at that content. Those are two different factors which together create a site with loyal, appreciative users. Just the sort of thing that every serious webmaster wants.

15.2 What Else Do We Know About Smart Pricing?

What Google has told us about Smart Pricing isn't much. It also raises at least as many questions as it answers: How does Google judge the quality of an ad? How can they tell the role an ad plays in a marketing campaign? What are the other "advertiser fluctuations"? And perhaps most importantly, how do they track the results of the clicks?

All of those pieces of information would be very useful to a publisher. But Google wasn't letting on.

Fortunately, publishers caught a break. Jennifer Sleg, the author of an excellent contextual advertising blog at www.Jensense.com, (you should definitely make this site a part of your regular reading) was contacted by an advertiser who was being tempted back from Yahoo! to Google. He told Jen what the AdSense salesman had told him about Smart Pricing. She told everyone else.

This is what it boiled down to:

- **Smart Pricing is calculated across an AdSense account.**
  So if you have a number of different sites covering a range of different topics and one of them delivers a low ROI, all of your ad prices may be lowered.

- **Smart Pricing is evaluated weekly.**
  If you believe that an ad is delivering a low ROI, you can remove it from your site and you should see higher ad prices within a week.

- **Smart pricing is tracked with a 30-day cookie.**

Users don't have to convert immediately into a sale (or whatever will count as a conversion) for you to benefit. They can think about it for a month and you'll still get the benefit.

- **Image ads are affected by smart pricing.**
  Few serious publishers use image ads except when they're receiving CPM campaigns. Was this a reference to ads in low locations receiving lower rates?
- **Prices may be reduced even below an advertiser's minimum bid.**
  So looking up the bid prices for targeted keywords won't help you very much; if your ROI is low, your rates could be lower than the minimum quoted.
- **Conversions accounts are tracked by advertisers opting into AdWords Conversion Tracking.**
  But we still don't know what Google is tracking or how it's making calculations with its results.

15.3 Strategies To Benefit From Smart Pricing

The challenge for publishers trying to keep their ad rates high is that there's no way to know exactly how many of your clicks are converting into sales for your advertisers. You can't even tell what would *count* as a sale for the different advertisers you're promoting.

The best you can do is keep track of your clicks and your revenues, and make sure that they rise and fall at the same rates.

If following your stats was always important, Smart Pricing has made it absolutely vital. There's little point in spending hours trying to increase your CTR if the value of your clicks is dropping like a rock.

So what should you do if you notice that your income is dropping but your CTR rate remains the same?

The first thing you should do is protect yourself. Because one site with a low ROI can affect all the sites in your account, dividing your sites between different accounts would prevent all of your revenues falling if one site underperforms. Officially, that's a breach of TOS, so you can't really do it. But I don't see why two different sites can't be owned by two spouses. If you own more than two sites though... well, I guess you're stuck.

Next, if you suspect that one page has a low ROI, try removing the AdSense code from that page, wait a week and see if you can spot an improvement in your ad prices. If there's no improvement, replace the code and try taking the code from a different page. You want to find the page that's poisoning your earnings and keep AdSense ads off it until you can bring in the kind of traffic that suits your advertisers.

And that's where you're most likely to find the underperforming pages. **The pages that are most likely to have the greatest conversion rates for advertisers are those that have the most loyal following.** The closer the connection between your site and the interests of your visitors the more likely they are to click on your ads — and buy when they click.

So it's also a good idea to create niche sites that appeal to niche audiences, rather than general sites that bring in audiences interested in a bunch of different things. Those sorts of users will also only have a vague interest in some of the things on your site and could lower your conversion rate.

You might have a blog, for example, in which you discussed your interests in dogs, computer games and the movies of Mel Gibson. That would bring in users with three different kinds of interests... and three different kinds of ads. But a dog-loving user who clicks on an ad for Mel Gibson DVDs is less likely to actually buy than a Mel Gibson fan. Your conversion rate would drop and the value of every ad you promote would fall too.

But if you created three separate blogs, one for each of your interests, you would receive fewer false clicks, and a higher rate of conversion.

Ultimately then, the ideal strategy is, as always, to create good content that attracts genuinely interested users.

> Don't remove the AdSense code from pages with low CTR; remove it from pages with low ROI!

16. HOW TO MAKE ADSENSE WORK WITH INTERNET COMMUNITIES AND COMMERCIAL SITES

Maximize your AdSense Revenue from Internet Forums, Message Boards and Discussion Groups!

Earlier in this book, I mentioned making revenue from blogs. But blogs certainly aren't the only types of content online or the only types that can use AdSense.

In an active Internet community, users generate most of the content.

You cannot completely control the keywords or the topics, which means AdSense might spring some surprises with the ads that show up. (Just have some Alternate Ads handy, in case AdSense pulls up a series of non-paying public service ads.)

Unlike passive surfers who like to explore your website for relevant information, forum members are very focused on their messages and the responses they attract.

Many publishers that play host to Internet communities complain of negligible CTRs, scattered keywords (low content relevance) and low cost per click. What they don't realize is that Internet communities are a hidden gold-mine which inspire fanatical loyalty, repeat visits, unique content and a high level of user involvement with the content.

Mega-brands such as Apple and Harley Davidson were built on the same foundation — a deep sense of personal bonding, high involvement with the product and strong referrals. You can achieve the same result with your website!

While all Internet communities are not the same, they do have the same key strengths. You just need to recognize them and find new ways to cash in on them — as some savvy web publishers are doing already!

16.1 Google's Forum Heat Map

Just as Google produced a heat map for standard websites, they've done the exact same thing for forums. You can find that map, together with their suggestions at adsense.blogspot.com/2005/10/six-adsense-optimization-tips-for.html.

On the whole, Google's tips are quite sensible. They suggest that a skyscraper on the left is a good idea and that horizontal ads should be placed beneath each forum entry. They also suggest putting a leaderboard at the bottom of the page, but before the footer, and opting in to take image ads.

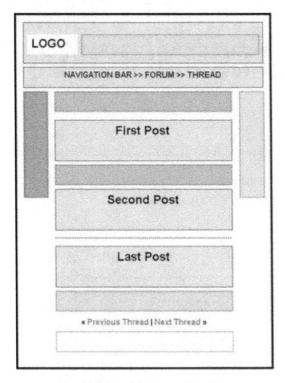

Fig. 15.1 Google's Forum Heat Map.

I'm not sure about all of those suggestions though. Here's why:

- Forum Members are very focused on their topic of discussion. **Ads that appear on the top, bottom or side margins of the page may not distract them from their main objective** — which is to read and write the posts!
  The best way to capture their attention is to **put your ads at the end of the top posting on each page.** Posts that appear on top are read more often, and usually set the tone for the rest of the discussion.
- Many web publishers swear by **Google's 728x90 leaderboard ad with two ads trailing top-of-the-page posts.**
- What gets the most clicks in any forum?
  The **forum buttons** of course! Put your ads close to these useful buttons, sought out by users to search threads, create a new thread or post a reply. Check out this example:

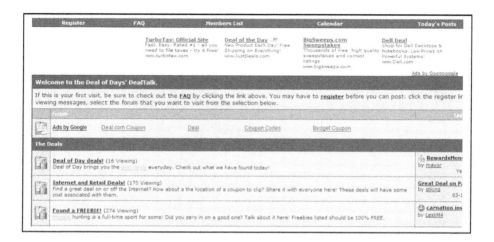

Fig. 15.2 Ad units on the DealofDay.com forum.

There are two kinds of ad units on this forum page at my site, DealofDay.com.

First, I've placed a leaderboard immediately beneath the navigation bar. It's impossible to miss there. Users have to look at the navigation bar and when they do, they'll see the ads.

But just look at the second ad unit. Can you see it? It's a horizontal link unit embedded in a space usually used to describe the thread.

I've even managed to make the "Ads by Google" line — which is usually a click-killer — match my thread titles. And because the ads are so relevant, there's a great chance they'll generate clicks. Even better, users on forums are used to clicking several times to get the content they need. They'll click on the general title of the forum thread, then the entries and the user profiles and so on.

That means that when they click on a link unit, there's a very good chance that they'll also click on the ads that turn up.

So that's two great ways to use ads on a forum: by placing them beneath the navigation bar; and by embedding them in the thread table.

There's another method though and it's so easy you'll be amazed that everyone isn't doing it...

Fig. 15.3 Spot The Deal of The Day.

Do you see that little title above the ad unit, the one that says "Deal Of Day"?

Without ever asking users to click, **the heading "Deal of Day" turns the Google Ads into a recommended resource for finding the day's top deals.**

Impressive forum stats, such as the number of members, threads and posts appear alongside the ads, making them look more legitimate. The sheer number of users creates a sense of urgency to check them out before other members get their hands on the coveted deals!

- Make sure you **apply the same text formatting as the user-generated content.** It's important to gain your users' attention first — then pitch your message when they're all ears!
- Try putting the ads **at the bottom of each post**. If users spot the pattern and your clickthroughs start to drop, try putting the ads at the bottom of every alternate post. The key is to keep them guessing!
- **Don't break up a post by putting ads in the middle.** Since forums have user-generated content, people are more sensitive to these intrusions and might be offended if you make the ads look like their personal recommendations.
- **Don't bunch ads together in the middle of the page.** It works well with 'passive' visitors, but your forum members will read right around them!
- **Allow users to pull up targeted ads with a Google Search Box!** How often has a forum posting piqued your interest enough to launch a Google search? Once? Twice? All the time? If you're anything like me, **the Google Search Box is an added convenience, welcomed by most users.** It makes your visitors stay! And if they click an ad from the results page, you make money!

Which of these strategies will work for your Forums?

Only time can tell so don't forget to track your results with Google's AdSense channels. There are publishers who have made a fortune with their community pages. It doesn't take rocket science. But a little persistence goes a long way!

17. WHAT TO DO BEFORE YOU APPLY TO GOOGLE ADSENSE — GUIDELINES FOR NEW WEB PUBLISHERS

Imagine this. Mr. Big Google Advertiser is surfing the net, looking up some trade-related keywords. He clicks through lazily to land on a strange website. The logo looks amateurish. The content is full of typos. Heck, some of the links don't even work. And then, he sees something he least expects to find.

He seems to freeze for a second. His eyes pop wide open and you can see a muscle going in his cheek. He picks up his phone and dials a number. "I can't believe it!" He booms, "I can't believe you put MY ad on THAT website!"

Uh oh.

Google has a reputation to live up to. A reputation for providing quality content, targeted traffic and good value for money to their advertisers.

The way to meet these requirements is to provide content that meets their requirements and goes one step further to add something unique, which other websites might not offer.

> Before you apply to Google AdSense, make sure you haven't cut corners on the layout and the quality of content. Google is quick to reject websites that are built specifically to attract search spiders or that trick people into clicking AdSense Ads.

To make a sizable income from AdSense, you need unique content, a true commitment to your visitors and **focused content** — which makes it easy for advertisers to target their audience.

To sum up, here are a few quick Do's and Don'ts before you apply:

17.1 Don't Build A Website That Targets Search Spiders And Have Nothing Unique To Offer Human Visitors

I've already discussed the importance of creating content that your users are genuinely going to find interesting. If you have interesting content, you'll have higher CTR and higher revenues.

With so many legitimate ways of creating revenue-generating content, you're only cheating yourself when you take a short-cut. You reduce your CTR and you increase the odds of being banned by Google.

17.2 Don't Build A Website Just To Make Money From AdSense

The easiest way to produce genuinely interesting content is to produce content that genuinely interests you!

You might feel that the more pages that you can throw up, the more money you'll make but if you can't produce the sort of content that can compete with companies who produce genuinely good material, you're not going to get the traffic or the revenues.

There are plenty of topics that you know about and enjoy. That's the kind of material that can give you money.

It will also make earning that money a lot more fun.

17.3 Provide Targeted Content That Will Help Google's Advertisers To Capitalize On Your Traffic

But writing about what you enjoy rather than what can help you earn doesn't mean you should forget about using your content to bring you targeted ads.

If you know that there are certain keywords in your topic that are worth more, then you can certainly write about those. You can also make sure that you toss in plenty of keywords and headings to keep those ads targeted.

17.4 DON'T Build A Website Specifically To Target High-Value Keywords Unless You Plan On Developing Quality Content!

Not all advertisers bid high on the same keywords.

Just as it's a bad idea to create more content simply to create more money, so it's a mistake to focus on particular keywords to create lots of money!

If you are prepared to produce good content and want that content to include high value keywords, one VERY useful report reveals those high-value keywords. You can find it at www.adsense-secrets.com/cashkeywords.html.

#	Keywords	Avg Bid	Searches	Results	R/S Ratio	Google Ads	CPD
1	new orleans real estate	$19.74	11,147	2,310,000	207	45	7.0
2	cleveland ohio real estate	$12.16	14,779	1,550,000	105	39	0.9
3	nashville real estate	$9.07	18,040	3,090,000	171	50 +	9.8
4	real estate license	$8.73	23,626	6,390,000	270	42	61.2
5	orlando real estate	$8.45	13,584	4,680,000	345	50 +	14.0
6	real estate lawyer	$7.75	13,414	9,740,000	726	38	8.2
7	real estate school	$7.22	37,674	16,300,000	430	46	52.2

Fig. 17.1 Sample report revealing high-value keywords.

If you want to aggressively build sites, another very useful tool you might want to look at is **Top Keyword Lists.**

This is a 'plug and play' monthly membership service offering twenty-five high-paying AdSense markets each and every week. With a simple page generating application, you can turn out twenty-five sites quickly and easily from each week's updates. If you prefer to spend a little more time building your site with articles, they offer a unique keyword research tool that allows you to pinpoint the key phrases you should concentrate your articles on for maximum payout through AdSense. Read more about it at www.adsenseaccelerator.com.

17.5 Do The SEO Thing

Websites that rank high in a Google search will earn more per-click than websites which rank lower for the same search term.

I don't know if that's because Google just wants to reward sites who meet their criteria for high search listings or because they assume that sites that rank higher are going to have better users for advertisers than lower-ranked sites.

Most likely though, is that it's all about content relevance.

A top-ranking website is considered more relevant than a lower-ranking one. So keep an eye on your Google search ranking for your targeted search terms and work continuously to optimize your website. The upshot is that when you've created your site, you need to pay attention to search engine optimization.

That won't only win you free traffic, it will also get you more money for the traffic you receive.

You can learn more about search engine optimization in chapter 22.

17.6 Increase 'Readiness To Buy'

Advertisers prefer websites that qualify visitors for the purchase. For example, a search for "cellphones" can throw up a page about the perils of cellphone radiation, a university professor's treatise about messaging technologies and a buyer's guide that compares features and prices of top-selling cellphone models.

For an advertiser looking to target cellphone buyers, the buyer's guide offers the most relevant (and therefore **valuable**) advertising space.

This is part of targeting your content.

You want people to click on your ads. So do your advertisers.

If you can keep your content focused on the products your advertisers are selling then you should be able to increase your CTR.

Of course, it's also Google's job to make sure that your ads match your content, but if you're writing about DVDs it makes sense to produce content that encourages people to buy DVDs because those are the sort of ads you know you're going to be served!

If you were writing about homebuying, you can be sure that you'd get ads about mortgages and real estate agents. Put up pages about finding the right mortgage or how to pick a real estate agent and not only do the ads look even more relevant, they'll also appear more attractive.

Fig. 17.2 **What the advertiser wants!** *Tim Carter is a living example of how content relevance builds loyalty. As an expert in his field, he adds relevance and credibility to the ads appearing on his pages. Check out this example at: www.askthebuilder.com/769_Hardwood_Floor.shtml.*

17.7 Don't Cut Corners!

Watch out for typos, amateurish layouts, malfunctioning links, poor-quality or plagiarized content.

Users expect to reach professional websites. Those are the ones they spend the most time on and pay the most attention to. Those are also the ones that Google rewards the most.

It pays to put effort into improving your website. It pays to have a good design and a site that's attractive and well-maintained.

Part 4

Advanced Tools
And Techniques

18. RECOMMENDED RESOURCES: TRY THESE TOOLS AND ADSENSE UTILITIES (SOME ARE FREE!)

MAKING LIFE EASIER FOR ADSENSE PARTNERS

18.1 Test Your Mettle With The Adsense Sandbox!

Before you apply to AdSense, put your web pages through a 'mock-test' with a FREE web utility called the AdSense Sandbox at www.digitalpoint.com/tools/adsense-sandbox. It's a great way to determine what type of ads your pages pull up. You can also estimate your earnings potential from the keywords in the ads.

The AdSense Sandbox is free to use, requires no subscription and displays results with a single click.

Many AdSense partners are already using it — with excellent results!

18.2 Google AdSense Preview Tool

If you have Windows Internet Explorer (version 6 or higher), you can install a neat tool provided by Google to check out ads that are most likely to show up on your web page.

To install the tool, click the second question in the list at www.google.com/adsense/support/bin/topic.py?topic=160 and follow the installation instructions.

You'll be able to check the destination of ads that are likely to appear on your site without being penalized for clicking your own ads, preview your color choices and see what geo-targeted ads are likely to show.

You might find that googleadspreview.blogspot.com does it better but if you use Explorer and only plan to use AdSense, Google's own tool certainly has its uses.

It takes just a few clicks and works with any Web page — even if you still haven't got AdSense.

18.3 Google AdWords Traffic Estimator and Bid Tool

If you are an AdWords advertiser, the Traffic Estimator will tell you the estimated bid price and traffic for your desired list of search terms. It's hugely useful and you can use it for free at adwords.Google.com/select/TrafficEstimatorSandbox.

19. KEEPING TRACK OF WHAT WORKS — AND WHAT DOESN'T WORK — FOR YOU!

People who want to lose weight often keep a "food diary". Without a food diary, it's easy to forget that late-night snack or the extra sugar in your fourth cup of coffee. A food diary keeps you honest. It helps you figure out the real reasons behind those little ups and downs in your weight.

I'm sure that after reading this book, you would be eager to try out many of the tweaks discussed in here — including some of your own, so...

Start an AdSense journal.

> Without an AdSense journal, it would be easy to undo your successes, or to repeat your failures. AdSenseDesktop provides everything you need to keep an ongoing journal of your AdSense activity!

Every little tweak counts, but don't try to do everything at once.

Take the step-by-step approach. Write your own AdSense plan for the first week. Log in to your AdSense account once a day to track your clickthroughs and earnings.

Don't be rigid about your plan. Make room for inspiration. If you've got a great idea, write it down to implement it later. Don't implement your ideas all at once and DO give every idea some time to prove its mettle. You'll find out within a day if you have thousands of visitors hitting your Web pages. If that is not the case, give it a few days. Preferably one week!

Don't be discouraged by minor, day-to-day fluctuations in your clickthroughs and earnings. It's normal and probably has nothing to do with your latest tweak.

Join an AdSense forum, several if possible. Share your tips with other members. Discuss what works and what doesn't work for you. Every once in a while, a forum member might alert you to a possible violation of the AdSense TOS. It could be just a false alarm, but I prefer to be safe than sorry!

When in doubt, dash an email to AdSense support, at adsense-support@Google.com.

Most emails are answered quickly by a real person. They won't suspend your account for asking them, but they might if you don't ask!

Read all you can and jot down every good idea. It will keep your interest levels high and give you something new to work on all the time.

Every new 'tweak' is your stepping stone to AdSense success.

Once you've reached a certain level, it's easy to say 'Cool! I've figured it all out!' But take it from me, Internet marketing keeps changing and the rules will change for you too.

Don't be like the two lazy little-people in "Who Moved My Cheese?" Keep looking for new ways to make money with AdSense. Replace ideas that no longer seem to work with new ideas and inspiration. Some people I know are still rubbing their backsides after the dot-com bust.

It's always easier when you see it coming than when it takes you by surprise! It doesn't matter how much money you've made with AdSense or what the IQ tests say about you: **It ain't working till your stats say so!**

19.1 *How To Keep An AdSense Journal*

For example, let's say you have a website about Bonsai trees. You read this book and you decide to start implementing the strategies that I've been talking about.

Your original stats might look something like this. You print these out and use them for comparison:

Date	Page Impressions	Clicks	Page CTR	Page eCPM	Your earnings
5/1/09	8020	160	2.0%	5.04	40.04
5/2/09	8186	172	2.1%	5.53	45.27
5/3/09	8071	153	1.9%	4.92	39.76
5/4/09	7792	156	2.0%	5.50	42.89
5/5/09	6712	154	2.3%	5.76	38.65
5/6/09	6596	132	2.0%	5.70	37.65
5/7/09	7134	157	2.2%	5.81	41.45

Clearly, your goal is going to be to lift up those CTRs, and by now you should have all sorts of ideas about how you're going to do that. You write down your first three:

- **3-Way Matching** — Text color, background and text size.
- **Layout** — Moving ads above the fold where they'll be most prominent.
- **Targeting ads** — Changing titles to improve relevancy and improving keywords.

You're already using 336 x 280 ads so you decide to start with 3-Way Matching and change all your ads so that they blend in with your page. You make the background color of the ads match the background color of your site and the font and color of the ad text the same as the font and color of your body text.

A week later, your stats look like this:

Date	Page Impressions	Clicks	Page CTR	Page eCPM	Your earnings
5/8/09	8123	236	2.9%	5.08	41.27
5/9/09	8135	244.05	3.0%	6.02	48.97
5/10/09	8024	249	3.1%	5.90	48.65
5/11/09	7926	238	3.0%	5.92	46.93
5/12/09	7865	252	3.2%	5.62	44.26
5/13/09	6645	193	2.9%	6.10	40.52
5/14/09	7103	220	3.1%	6.06	43.05

Already your weekly incomes have risen from $285.71 to $313.65 and your average CTR has gone up by a full percentage point. That's a good start, but you've still got a fair way to go.

You print out this week's report and write next to it "3-Way Matching" so that you know exactly what you did to create those changes. Now you know how much 3-Way Matching is worth to your incomes.

Next, you move the ads that you have at the bottom of your pages to the areas above the fold and place them in prominent positions. A week later, you print out the following stats:

Date	Page Impressions	Clicks	Page CTR	Page eCPM	Your earnings
5/15/09	8365	343	4.1%	5.93	49.65
5/16/09	8296	324	3.9%	6.04	50.09
5/17/09	8032	321	4.0%	6.42	51.59
5/18/09	7920	317	4.0%	6.30	49.93
5/19/09	7853	306	3.9%	6.20	48.67
5/20/09	6725	282	4.2%	6.68	44.92
5/21/09	7145	293	4.1%	6.51	46.55

Again, your CTR has risen by another percentage point and your weekly income has gone up to $341.40. Next to this set of stats, you write "Layout" and you place them in your journal after your second set.

Now things are getting a little trickier. Your ads are blended onto the page and they're in prominent positions. But you find that they aren't always showing the most relevant ads. On your page on growing bonsai from cuttings for example, you find that you're getting lots of ads about scrapbooking. A look at your server logs supports your hunch that these aren't getting any clicks at all.

You create a channel for that page and follow your stats for a week. The original stats look like this:

Channel	Ad Unit Impressions	Clicks	Ad Unit CTR	Ad Unit eCPM	Your earnings
Cuttings page	829	8	1.0%	1.44	1.20
Cuttings page	764	9	1.2%	1.89	1.44
Cuttings page	801	7	0.9%	1.22	0.98
Cuttings page	712	7	1.0%	1.37	0.98
Cuttings page	758	10	1.3%	1.85	1.40
Cuttings page	652	5	0.8%	1.07	0.70
Cuttings page	704	6	0.9%	1.19	0.84

That's pretty weak but as few of your users are likely to be interested in scrapbooking, it's not too surprising. So you change the title of the page from www.bonsai.com/cuttings.html to www.bonsai.com/tree_cuttings.html and turn the word "cuttings" into "tree-cuttings," especially in the area beneath the ad box.

You upload, wait for the robot to index your page again and check that you're now getting ads from gardening and horticulture sites.

After a week, you find that your stats for that page look like this:

Channel	Ad Unit Impressions	Clicks	Ad Unit CTR	Ad Unit eCPM	Your earnings
Cuttings page	1300	52	4.0%	6.40	8.32
Cuttings page	1423	58	4.1%	6.52	9.28

Cuttings page	1346	52	3.9%	6.18	8.32
Cuttings page	1256	50	3.9%	6.40	8.04
Cuttings page	1156	44	3.8%	6.09	7.04
Cuttings page	1098	45	4.0%	6.56	7.20
Cuttings page	1247	49	3.9%	6.29	7.84

Again, you'd want to print out this page and place it in your journal.

So far in the last three weeks, these simple tweaks would have already increased your weekly income by over $104.

And there's still plenty more you can do!

You can make sure that every page is optimized, you can look for higher-paying keywords and you can experiment with different colors and layouts, search boxes and multiple ads to increase your revenues.

And of course, you can create more pages and more sites.

Note that only in the last example (when you changed the keywords, improving your position in the search engines) did any of the changes affect your impressions. These tweaks simply made the most of the traffic you already have!

Of course, if you add more traffic, you'll make more money.

The important point to remember is that you should be recording everything you do and keeping a close eye on the results. Within a few weeks, you'll have a complete record of all the changes you've made and what they're worth to your bottom line.

20. OTHER CONTEXTUAL ADVERTISING PROGRAMS AND HOW TO USE THEM WITH ADSENSE

AdSense is probably the easiest way to generate revenue with your website — I know it's making me a fantastic amount of money — but it's certainly not the only way you can make money using contextualized advertising.

At the beginning of 2007, Google changed its Terms of Service to allow publishers to place other contextualized ad systems on the same pages as AdSense units. There's just one restriction: those other systems' ads can't look like AdSense units.

That still leaves you a huge range of possibilities.

In this chapter, I'm going to look at some of the other programs that you could use — either instead of AdSense or as well as AdSense. I'll explain how they work and how you can make them work with AdSense.

20.1 Kontera — Making Your Words Pay

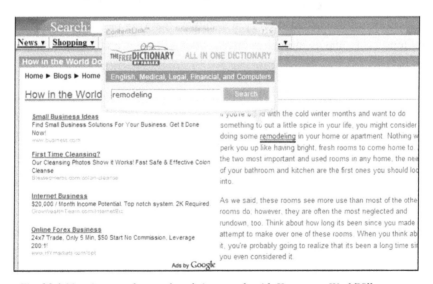

Fig. 20.1 Mousing over keywords to bring up ads with Kontera at WorldVillage.com.
Note how Kontera and AdSense complement each other here.

Kontera (www.kontera.com) is a great way to make extra revenue. Instead of putting ad units on your site like AdSense does, Kontera highlights particular keywords in your text and brings up an ad when the user mouses over them.

The words are marked out from regular links by two underlines, and you can change the colors of the text and the links. For some of the biggest publishers, the ad inventory even includes some very high-earning video ads.

I use Kontera on my site WorldVillage.com and I've been pretty impressed with the results. The ads are fun to bring up, they're relevant and they're totally unobtrusive.

But like AdSense, you will need to play with them to maximize your revenues. There are so many different factors that affect your incomes with Kontera, such as **which keywords you want highlighted**, **where you want those words to appear** on the page and **which colors to choose** for the best results, that it took me some time to figure out all of the best combinations.

It also took me a few phone calls directly to the people who'd created it to get an idea of what happens behind the scenes of the program so that I can maximize my income.

The key issues are the number of links you should place on your Web pages, the color of the links and how those links are distributed.

The first issue is pretty simple. Kontera lets you place up to six ad links on each page and recommends that you take all of them.

I don't see any reason to argue with that. In general, your best strategy when building a website that earns income through advertising is to keep the pages relatively short and focused on just one topic. That will keep your ads relevant. If you're following that strategy, it's unlikely that your page is going to look overstuffed with Kontera's ads. You'll probably find no more than three or four on a page, and because they only appear as links they won't distract the user.

The color of the links is a tougher question. Usually, it's best to choose a different color to the one you've used for your AdSense units. That's because Google and Kontera tend to pick up on different keywords. Offering different links in different colors helps to emphasize that variety and lets Kontera's links stand out.

If you're thinking that the goal of optimization is to blend the ads into your site, you're right. But these links are going to be *embedded* in your content. They're also going to be double-underlined so that they'll look different anyway. You want people to see them and to place their mouse over them.

You could try using blue as your link color if you want. I use them sometimes on my blog. But I suspect that if you tested different colors, you might well find that a tone that matches your site's design will give you better results. Testing is going to be key.

Making sure that the ads appear in the best locations on the page is easy to do but might require a little work. For the most part, Kontera's software should distribute the ads fairly evenly across the page. But if you want to make sure that you don't get any ads in particular places on the page, you can use Zone Tags. These simply tell Kontera: "No ads here please."

To define certain text areas as off-limit simply add the line:

```
<span name=KonaFilter>
```
before the text, and the tag:

```
</span>
```
at the end.

If that sounds to you like AdSense's Section Targeting, you're on the right track. But Kontera's filters aren't exactly the same as Section Targeting. Placing these filter tags won't prevent Kontera's contextualization engine from checking that section for keywords. The contents of that section will still be used to assess the meaning of the Web page. Kontera just won't place ads on any keywords it finds there.

While that's useful for keeping ads away from the bottom of the page, the sidebars or spots right next to AdSense units, you can also use the tags to control which terms are highlighted.

Kontera doesn't let you choose which terms and phrases you want turned into ads. But it does recommend that you make the phrases you use as specific as possible. Talking about the "Nokia 5300 XpressMusic myFaves Black Phone" from T-Mobile is likely to get you better ads and more clicks than talking about "mobile phones."

There are a lot of different strategies that you can use with Kontera. Far too many for me to describe in detail here. That's why I put them together in a short book that lets other publishers can shorten their learning curve. You can find that book at www.konterasecrets.com.

If you're going to put Kontera on your site in addition to AdSense — and I can't think of a single reason why you shouldn't — you will need that book to shoot straight to the high revenues.

20.2 Intellitxt's Eye-Catching Ads

Fig. 20.2 Intellitxt's video ads grab your attention.

Intellitxt is a direct rival to Kontera. The company's system works in a similar way: by picking keywords, turning them into links and producing floating ads when users mouse over.

When Kontera was first rolled out it was probably fair to say that Intellitxt was at least as good, if not better. Their ads looked great (Kontera's were a bit bland initially) and they turned up some very good ads.

These days I'm not so sure. The people at Kontera have put so much work into improving their contextualization engine that Intellitxt certainly doesn't have an edge there. In fact, you can often find that the ads will match the keyword but the keywords won't be the most relevant terms on the page.

Nor can you define the link color, which is stuck on green or be certain that an ad will contain an image, the most attractive part of these sorts of floating ads.

What you might get though is a movie. And those movies are great. Unlike Google's video ads, these start automatically and they're impossible to miss.

Unfortunately, they're only for really big sites. If you have fewer than 500,000 page views a month, you don't qualify. That's a shame because some advertisers have reported CTRs two and three times higher for these ads than for AdSense ads. And you can be sure they're paying a lot more too.

If you do have lots of users though — or think you will soon — those video ads might have been a good reason to choose Intellitxt over Kontera, but Kontera has now produced its own line of rich media ads. (Although again you need to be big to benefit from them.)

The same placement and keyword strategies that work with Kontera should work with Intellitxt too but I'd always turn to Kontera first. It's the system that I use on my blog. First thing you'll want to do is get signed up at www.adsense-secrets.com/kontera.html.

20.3 Chitika Premium — Different Ads for Different Users

Kontera and Intellitxt all fit so neatly into your site, you'll hardly notice the difference to your page.

You will notice the difference in your revenues though.

Chitika's Premium units are more intrusive than text links but that's not necessarily a bad thing. One of their greatest advantages is that they are just so well-targeted... especially to users most likely not just to click but to buy.

Fig. 20.3 Chitika's Premium ads. A trip!

Chitika's old ad units — its eMiniMalls — looked great. They attracted eyes, drew attention and as long as they were placed on a site related to products, they brought clicks too.

Unfortunately, if you didn't have a site related to products, they didn't generate a lot of clicks. Worse, many of the clicks they did generate didn't result in sales. So the advertisers started getting uppity and they demanded Chitika provide ads that produce conversion rates — not clickthrough rates, conversion rates! — of at least 2 percent.

Enter Chitika Premium. These show a list of ads, a little image next to each link and a search tab that allows users to look for other ads if they want. Like AdSense (and the old eMiniMalls) they pay on a CPC basis, so each click gives cash, and they're compatible with AdSense too so you can use both types of units on the same page.

So far, so familiar. But here's the big important difference…

The ads are only shown to select users.

Chitika chose to increase conversion rates for its advertisers not by better matching its ads to all of a site's users, but by not showing the ads to people who are unlikely to buy.

So users will only see a Chitika Premium ad unit if they:

- Are based in the United States or Canada;
- And reach the site from a search engine.

That second condition is really important. Chitika Premium targets its ads by looking at the term the user entered into the search engine. A user who didn't enter the site through a search engine hasn't entered a keyword term, so Chitika can't target its ads.

But that immediately excludes a large chunk of your users.

In fact, it cuts out *all of your regular users*.

While it's important as a publisher to keep new users coming in, it's even more important to keep your old users coming back. That will give you a community of users who are keen to read your content, who will constantly see your AdSense units and who will follow the recommendations you make, helping you earn from affiliate products.

Chitika isn't interested in those users though. It's only interested in your brand new users, the ones who have stumbled through to your site after looking at a search engine for the type of content you offer.

That might sound like a terrible idea. You want everyone to see your ads, not just a select few. But it has turned out be a smart move. Publishers who have used Chitika Premium units — and optimized them — have typically reported overall earnings as much as 25 percent higher than using AdSense alone.

That's not going to happen for every publisher though. **For one, it can only happen for sites that have good search engine optimization.**

If your site appears somewhere on page seventeen of the search results for anyone looking for your main keyword and if search traffic makes up only a tiny fraction of your users, then you're not going to make much money with Chitika.

Very few people will see the ads.

Instead of seeing Chitika's Premium ads, they'll either see a replacement unit that you've created or they'll see nothing at all. The ad unit will simply collapse and it will be as though there was never anything on that spot on the page.

Or to put it another way, instead of placing a valuable ad on a prime piece of website real estate, you'll be offering nothing... and earning nothing.

So it's not just important to have a lot of search traffic to earn from Chitika. **You'll also need to make good use of the company's alternate URL service so that you're *always* earning from that ad spot.**

This works in the same way as AdSense's alternatives to public service ads. You'll need to create a Web page with the content you want to show in that space and enter the URL in the Alternate URL box.

You've got three options here. The easiest is to paste your AdSense code onto an empty page, place it on your server and use the URL of that page as your alternate. Just make sure that you use the same ad format as the Premium ad.

Chitika insists that AdSense is smart enough to recognize that it's being used as an alternate ad. It will take its context as the page on which the viewer sees it, not the blank page you placed it on.

US and Canadian users who come through a search engine will see the Chitika ad; everyone else will see an AdSense unit.

The second option is to use an affiliate product.

In general, affiliate ads work best when you've recommended the product. Place an ad for a wetsuit on your Web page about diving, for example, and maybe a few people will click through. Place the same ad on a page in which you describe how that suit kept you warm while you were photographing penguins and anyone thinking of diving in cold water won't just click through, they'll buy it — and you'll get a share of the revenue.

For affiliate ads to be really effective then, the user has to have read your content. That's why they often work best when embedded in an article rather than placed at the top of the page where AdSense units often do well.

Embed a Chitika unit into your content and a new user who just glances at your page and considers clicking away will see a list of search-based ads. Regular readers who are familiar with your content and the products you recommend will see your affiliate ad.

You'll be offering two different kinds of ads for two different kinds of users in the same place.

And you can assign a CPM ad as your alternate URL as well.

That will make sure that you get paid for everyone who sees it, but because not everyone will see it — and you always need a lot of traffic to make the most of CPM ads — you'll need a huge amount of traffic to benefit from a CPM ad as a Chitika Premium alternate.

Which of these methods would work best for you?

Only testing will tell.

Offering different ads to different types of users means that the differences between sites can produce a huge range of results even for sites using the same approach.

If you rarely recommend products, for example, then you might find that using AdSense as your alternate will produce higher revenues than an affiliate ad. If your site has a lot of clickthrough traffic however, then placing a CPM ad might be best.

You'll have to try each type of alternate in turn, check the results and see which option works best for you.

And much too will depend on where you place the units.

Not surprisingly, Chitika recommends placing its ads above the fold and ideally, near the title of your content. One publisher has reported a great deal of success by placing two units right at the top of the page so that they're the first thing the user sees: an AdSense unit; and next to it, a Chitika Premium unit with an AdSense alternate.

The fact that that strategy has produced higher earnings than two AdSense units together suggests something about the power of these units: for the kinds of users that Chitika targets, these ads were more attractive than AdSense's units. A user from the US or Canada who reached the page through a search engine was more likely to click a Chitika unit than an AdSense unit in the same place.

Would that be the same for your site?

That's an easy strategy to test. Run two AdSense units together for a week then swap one of those units for a Chitika Premium unit with an AdSense alternate and compare your earnings.

If you find that you're earning more with a Chitika unit, you'll have picked up some valuable information about the behavior of one subset of your users.

You'll know they're more likely to click these ads than AdSense units. You'll be able to offer them those Chitika ads they love and you'll still be able to serve regular AdSense units to everyone else.

That's one very easy and valuable strategy you can — and probably should — test on your site.

Another is to use a Chitika banner with a CPM ad alternate and place it at the top of the page.

Banner ads that pay on a CPM basis are a bit old school but lots of publishers do still use them. Users tend to look right past them even though that spot, right at the top of the page, should be very valuable. Placing a Chitika unit there might allow you to continue earning from your less valuable users on a CPM basis while making better use of that prime site for the sorts of users advertisers want the most.

On the other hand, if you have lots of AdSense units lower down on the page, you might find that your revenues fall as you lose CPM earnings, and users who would have clicked an ad embedded in the content click a Chitika ad at the top of the page instead. You'll just be changing the place they click the ad. Again, you won't know until you've tried both approaches and compared the results.

In general, the rules governing placement of Chitika's units are the same as those for AdSense units: blend the ads into the page but make them unmissable by putting them above the fold and where eyeballs will be looking.

The most important question you'll have to answer is what the alternate ad should be and whether you wouldn't do better just by offering everyone an AdSense unit. The answer might be different for every site but with a little time and a little effort, it's a question that every publisher can answer.

A tougher question concerns keywording. Although Google provides very few tools to help publishers influence the ads they receive, as we've seen, there are a number of things you can do to bring up more valuable links. Chitika's ads however are prompted by a user's search term. You can't influence that, but you can influence whether your site appears in a search engine listing for that term.

Chitika's Premium ads make it more important than ever to keyword your site comprehensively for search engines. Even if your content only has a loose attachment to a keyword, it could now be a good idea to make sure that a search engine returns your site for it. The user might not be too interested in your content but he could be interested in the ad that he receives *above* the content.

Adding and optimizing those keywords will take effort — a lot more effort than testing different alternate ads and deciding whether Chitika or AdSense delivers the best returns in a certain spot. But if you're prepared to put the work into search engine optimization, you might find that you get some interesting results from users you wouldn't otherwise have seen.

To look at, Chitika's Premium ads appear to offer little new. In fact, it's what they don't offer that makes them so interesting. By showing different ads to different types of users, they could allow publishers to make the most money from everyone.

At the very least, they make it easier to A/B test your most valuable users.

You can learn more about Chitika at www.ChitikaSecrets.com.

20.4 Yahoo! Publisher Network

Yahoo! Publisher Network is probably the number one competitor to Google. In fact, Yahoo! pretty much copied what AdSense had done... but didn't do it quite as well.

On the plus-side, the ad formats are largely the same. So if you need to switch from AdSense to YPN, you should be able to keep the exact same optimization, at least as regards how the ads look (although YPN doesn't have Ad Links or Search, so you'd lose those.)

And the RSS ads, which were a big advantage until Google rolled out its own, were cancelled at the beginning of 2009.

As to which ads you get served though, that's a whole other ball game. One of the biggest problems with YPN is that the first ads it serves are often Run-Of-The-Network (RON) ads, Yahoo!'s answer to public service ads. These are just ads for companies that seem to have struck a special deal with YPN.

They pay well, when you get a click out of them, but they're not contextualized so you don't get many clicks. They occur much more frequently than public service ads and they're much harder to get rid of.

And there are no CPM ads on Yahoo!, which can be a good thing or a bad thing depending on the size of your site and your experience.

Most publishers find that they get better results with AdSense than they do with YPN... although we all keep a close eye on YPN to see if they improve enough to attract us.

20.5 AdBrite

Google's big thing is serving contextual ads. Its program checks the content of your site and delivers ads that it thinks your users will like. AdBrite is much simpler.

The idea behind AdBrite is that people tend to ask popular sites to advertise their links. You've probably had that happen to you. Instead of asking for a link in return though, you could ask for money.

AdBrite is a clearing house for sites that want to sell advertising space on their pages and for advertisers who want to choose where they want to place their ads.

For advertisers, the advantage over Google is that they know exactly where their ads are appearing and for exactly how much money each time.

Publishers — like you — get to set your own ad rates, and you have the right to approve or reject every ad before it's placed on your site. That gives you the power to choose your ads and your price instead of relying on whatever Google gives you.

Those are the advantages. The disadvantages are that it's just not in the same league as AdSense... or even YPN.

You can learn more about AdBrite at www.adbrite.com.

20.6 Kanoodle – Bright Ads

 The same criticism can be made of Kanoodle's BrightAds service, which is similar to Google's. It's a search engine that delivers contextual ads to publishers' websites.

The contextualizing isn't quite as accurate as Google's but BrightAds does offer a number of options that Google doesn't offer — or at least not yet. Its RSS advertising program has been around for a while, it has a focus on local sites which might be attractive to businesses with local markets (or sites with content of local interest) and it also serves ads related to previous user behavior. If a user visits a lot of real estate sites, for example he could continue to receive ads about real estate even if he's on a site about sport. That means your site could be displaying ads that have nothing to do with your content.

That's all creative stuff and it's nice to see new ideas. It would be nicer though to see revenues that compete with Google's and I haven't heard of anyone earning more with BrightAds than they can earn with Google.

Learn more about Kanoodle's BrightAds at www.kanoodle.com.

20.7 Searchfeed

Searchfeed is slightly better, especially for international publishers. It also supplies contextualized ads to advertisers but offers geotargeting services which gives them a wide global reach, useful if you're based outside the United States.

You can integrate the ads smoothly into your site, either by cutting and pasting the HTML from SearchFeed's site or even by asking the company's own specialists to help you increase your CTR. And it has a good reputation for paying on time.

Whether SearchFeed will give you more money than Google is a different question though. The only way to find that out is to try it but if you find that you're doing well with Google, then why would you bother?

If, for some reason, you don't want to use Google — or can't use Google — and YPN isn't your cup of tea either, then you might find Searchfeed a good alternative.

You can learn more about Searchfeed at www.searchfeed.com.

20.8 The Big Boys: eBay And Microsoft

One of the great things about contextualized advertising is that outside of Google and Yahoo!, the best competitors are all start-ups. Or should that be up-starts?

A couple of big boys though have begun to muscle in on the market.

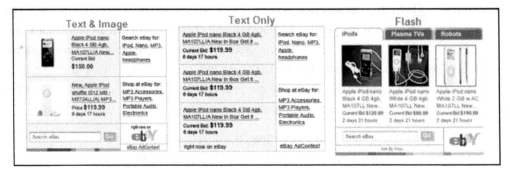

Fig. 20.4 eBay's ad selections.

eBay now has its own contextualized affiliate system. The system scans publishers' Web pages, identifies keywords and serves related ads drawn from its online auctions. Publishers receive between 40 and 70 percent of eBay's commission on the sale.

These ads aren't embedded into text. They appear in units, like AdSense ads. And like AdSense ads, you're free to change the color scheme and ad size, and place the code wherever you want.

But they're always going to look like ads. When the most eyecatching part of the ad is the price, there's no hiding the fact that any user who clicks is heading to a sales page and not to a site that will give him information.

And because the ads will change with the auctions, unless you're writing specifically about a product that someone is always selling at eBay, you'd probably do better promoting new goods with an Amazon affiliate ad.

That's especially true as long as eBay make it difficult for people to join the program. The system is currently only available to eBay's affiliates. But you can become an affiliate at www.affiliates.ebay.com and check out the ad program at affiliates.ebay.com/ads/adcontext/index.html.

The other big company stepping into the field is Microsoft. It's been talking about rolling out a contextualized ad system for a long time but only really got going in 2006.

It's still far behind.

There's nowhere for publishers to sign up at the moment (it's invitation only), the ads are only running on MSN's own network and the inventory looks pretty limited.

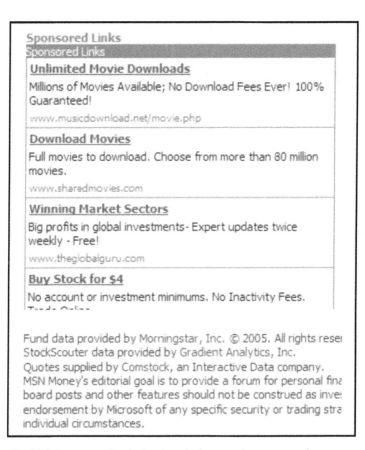

Fig. 20.5 A contextualized ad unit at the bottom of moneycentral.msn.com.

Although we know that the system is going to use demographic and geo-targeting to keep the ads close to users, that advertisers can choose keywords and will pay per click, we know nothing about how the contextualization system is actually going to work. Some of the results turning up on some of MSN's sites are way off.

What we do know though is that the ad units are going to look a lot like AdSense units.

If Microsoft can build up advertisers and iron out the bugs, they could be a good alternative to Google and YPN. Until then though, it's still AdSense plus text links and affiliate ads.

20.9 A Comprehensive Ad Strategy For Your Website

You can see then that there's no shortage of options available for publishers looking to monetize their websites. AdSense will always be the foundation. I've probably used just about every ad system out there and whenever something new comes out, I test it to breaking point to see what it can do for me.

I still haven't found anything that comes close to generating the sort of cash that AdSense makes for me.

But that doesn't mean I only use AdSense on my websites.

In fact, I believe that every website should use three different kinds of ads: CPC ads; CPM ads; and affiliate ads.

It's a bit like loading a fishing rod with three different kinds of bait at the same time.

Users who see a CPC ad they like will click, generating a small amount of revenue for you.

Recommend an affiliate product on your Web page and some users will buy, giving you a useful commission.

And all of your users will contribute towards your CPM revenues, even if each only brings in a few cents.

You don't want to load your pages with so many ads that you overwhelm the content. But you do want to make sure that you turn as many of your users into cash as you possibly can.

One strategy then is to place a CPM banner ad right at the top of the page, above the navigation bar. Users have grown used to seeing banners up there and barely glance at them. Very few will click them so placing a CPC ad — such as an AdSense unit — is often a bit of a waste. But even a quick glance can have branding power for a company, and they're prepared to pay to put their name in front of users.

You can then embed your AdSense units into your content, perhaps with a secondary, word-based CPC system such as Intellitxt, and place an affiliate ad in a sidebar.

Managing three different kinds of ad systems though can be challenging. You might be working with four different companies, making following your stats difficult. The more companies you use, the greater the number of different ways of arranging your ads, making testing longer and more complex.

And, of course, you might also want to sell advertising space on your page directly which means you'll need to know how much each type of page is worth, the values of different locations on the page and the availability of those spots so that you can take bookings and know how much to charge advertisers.

That's all tricky stuff, which is why Google rolled out a solution…

20.10 Comprehensive Ad Strategies The Easy Way With Google Ad Manager

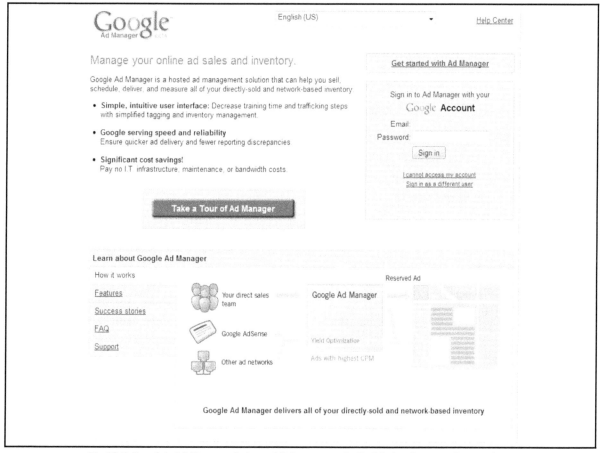

Fig 20.6 Google's Ad Manager helps publishers control all of their ad systems in one place.

Google's Ad Manager is a fantastic tool. Its main goal is to help publishers who wish to sell space on their sites directly to advertisers. It does that by keeping track of the number of impressions your pages generate and are likely to generate in the future.

It can even help you to sell packages of ad slots so that advertisers can easily place their ads in multiple locations on your site.

It's all fairly complex stuff and is really aimed at websites that are well-established — or at least established enough for competing advertisers to see the value of placing their ads on the sites' pages.

But Ad Manager does a little more than that.

Forget about the feature that allows publishers to fill unsold space with AdSense units. It's likely that most of the ad spots on your website will contain AdSense units anyway while directly sold units will be the occasional cherry on the cake.

Instead, look at the Ad Network Management feature. This lets you track ads from different networks. Rather than having to log in separately to all of the different companies who are supplying your ads, you'll be able to go to one place and pick up all of the figures together.

That's all very useful but using Ad Manager to do this does have one big advantage.

As I said, Ad Manager is really aimed at fairly big websites. It's used by sites as large as The Nation and Date.com. It might take you while to build your website to a size like that and in the meantime, many of Ad Manager's features — such as its ability to keep track of the value of multiple ad slots and make them available to advertisers — might be of little use.

But knowing they're there will give you something to aim at. You'll know that the next stage of growing your Internet business is to skip the third party providers, sell directly to competing advertisers and keep all of the revenues for yourself.

When you know where you're going next, there's a much better chance you'll get there.

And having played around with Ad Manager as you make the journey, you'll be ready when you arrive.

21. GETTING TRAFFIC TO YOUR WEB SITE

One of the most frequent questions I am asked is "Will your ebook teach me how to get more traffic to my web site?" Lots of people have written books — and series of books — on generating traffic. The focus of *this* ebook is to show you how to maximize the traffic that you already have. And while tips for building pages through forums and free content are excellent ideas, they are no replacement for a solid course on how to get more people to visit your site. Because this question is so common though, I will address it briefly in this chapter. I'll give you the basics, describe some unusual ideas that some people are using and tell you where you can get all the information you need.

In the next chapter, you'll also find a quick run-through of search engine optimization.

21.1 Advertising

Let's start with the obvious: buying advertising. We've already talked about AdWords/AdSense arbitrage but exactly the same principle applies to buying your traffic from other sources too.

For example, for a long time, the minimum price for advertising at Overture —now owned by Yahoo! — was ten cents per click and you had to spend at least $20 each month. If you could see that the ads being served on your site were generating less than ten cents per click then you were never going to make a profit.

Exactly the same is true of any other pay-per-click advertising campaign.

One of the advantages of following your AdSense stats is that you can estimate how much the clicks on your ads are worth. That can tell you how much you can afford to pay for clicks from other sites when you buy advertising.

It might well pay to advertise, but before you buy make sure it pays a profit.

21.2 Reciprocal Linking

Many people focus on linking in order to improve their search engine rankings. That's important but don't forget that the links themselves can be one of your biggest sources of traffic!

Probably the easiest way to invite links (apart from searching out related sites and writing to each one) is to add a "link" section to your pages where webmasters can choose a banner, button or text link to place on their site. On the same page, they can also submit their own site for linking. That should help you swap links without being swamped by sites looking for free placement.

The most critical factor when requesting a link though is where the site places it. Links on the home page always do better than a link buried on one of the internal pages and a good banner or graphic link on a site with content related to yours will usually get more clicks than a text link.

If you find that your links aren't appearing on the pages you want, there are a couple of simple remedies that you can use.

The first is to ask for a better position! If you have a good relationship with the webmaster or if it's a small site, there's a good chance that they'll agree. It certainly won't hurt to ask.

Not everyone is so generous though, and another option is to offer something in return. A link in a similar position on your own site can make a good deal if your sites are of similar size but you can also offer content or even a special page for that site's users.

If you have a site about furniture for example, and you want a link at a top directory for home furnishings then you could create a special welcome page for users of that site to draw them deeper into yours and deliver targeted ads. You might even want to go as far as creating a sort of co-branded version of your site for their users to click into. As long as you're getting paid when the users click on the ads, what do you care whose design they're looking at?

21.3 Send A Friend

There's nothing like viral marketing to promote your site! It's free, it comes with trusted recommendations and it gives you great CTR.

Each of your content pages should have a link marked "Send a friend" which opens a form so that the user can send your URL onwards. Until Google allows ads in email, there's little point in AdSense members sending actual content but there's no reason why you (or your users) can't send links to pages with ads.

21.4 Offline Marketing

One of the biggest mistakes that people make when they build an Internet business is to forget that there's a world outside the Internet! Just because you make money out of traffic doesn't mean you have to source all of that traffic online.

You should make sure that your URL is listed on all of your marketing material: your business cards, Yellow Pages ads, flyers, envelopes, freebies and just about anything else you can think of.

You should certainly have your site address in your email signatures.

21.5 Promoting Your Blog

I've talked quite a bit about blogging in this book, mostly because I know from experience that it's possible to make a very nice income from a good blog but also because a lot of people aren't making the most of the blogs they have.

If you've got AdSense on your blog, there's a whole range of different things that you can easily do to increase your traffic and earn extra cash.

The first thing you should do is make sure that your blog is set to ping rpc.pingomatic.com as soon as you've updated. Pingomatic.com offers a free all-in-one pinging service that covers all the large blog directories and search engines. On Blogger.com, you can find this in your settings; other blog tools, such as Movable Type and Wordpress have a similar option.

You should also set up an RSS feed to let people know when you update. Apart from the fact that you can now place ads on your feeds, it will also keep your regular users coming back to see more ads (and to see your latest posts).

Instead of linking to the previous month's or the previous week's posts, each page should also have its own link. Sounds obvious, right? And yet how many blogs have you seen with one link to about twenty different entries? One link per entry means more pages for ads, better links from external sites and higher search engine rankings.

You should certainly comment on other people's blogs, especially those that write about the same sort of things as your site, but ultimately the best way to get traffic to your blog is to make it good. If your writing is dull or difficult to read, it doesn't matter how hard you push it, no one will want to read it — and those who do stay won't stick around to click the ads.

21.6 Public Relations And Publicity

Just about all of the methods that you use to bring people to your site will cost you money. You'll have to pay for ads on other sites, you'll have to give up valuable real estate on your site to lists of links and you'll have to decide how much you want to pay for an AdWords campaign.

Publicity can be free.

It doesn't have to be, of course. You can pay a PR expert to publicize your site for you and place articles in the press on your behalf... but it's not necessary and they can be too expensive for most sites, especially at the beginning.

Or you can simply create a good quality press release yourself, fax it out to the media and wait for reporters to call.

Sound difficult?

It really isn't. A press release is just one page and will take between twenty and forty minutes to write.

There are a number of rules you have to follow: you need a gripping headline; you have to include a quote; and you have to be available for the interview to name just three. Most importantly though you have to have a story the press wants to run.

Telling them that you've just launched a new site isn't going to cut it. Telling them that your new site is going to set a new trend or change some people's lives just might.

Think about the effect that your piece of "news" will have on the public and you've got the beginnings of a great story.

And what do you get in return for doing that? Well, not only do you get the name of your business in the press, you also get the halo that comes with it. When you're in the media, people assume that you're an expert. You become the number one source for whatever your website offers.

And to underline that fact, you can even put a button on your home page that says something like: "As Seen On CNN!"

Sound good?

The real expert on marketing through free publicity is Paul Hartunian. This is the guy who bought a hunk of wood that had been removed from the Brooklyn Bridge during renovations, cut it into one-inch cubes and wrote a press release with the headline "New Jersey Man Sells Brooklyn Bridge For $19.95."

He was on CNN for two days and the story was run as far away as Peru.

He now lives on a 30-acre estate and teaches people how to use publicity for their businesses. You can order his publicity kit at www.hartunian.com.

21.7 Generating Traffic With Social Media Sites

I've saved the best method till last.

When I first started in online marketing, generating traffic wasn't just the biggest challenge of making money with websites, it was also the biggest headache.

Although there have always been lots of different strategies available, not all of them are fun.

That's just not true any more.

In fact, social networking is probably the most effective way of bringing in new users and turning your existing users into a community.

And it's also the kind of thing that you'd be happy to do just because it's so enjoyable.

The two sites that I use to promote my online business are Facebook and Twitter.

There are plenty of other options available. MySpace, for example, has gazillions of members. But I haven't found that it can deliver particularly good traffic. If you're a teenager looking for a way to find free music, MySpace might be a good service. But for most Internet entrepreneurs, it's just not going to be very effective.

LinkedIn is good too. If you're looking for a job, then keeping in touch with people you once studied with or worked alongside is certainly useful but LinkedIn's groups can also be a great way to target business-minded people.

Facebook though has turned out to be very effective.

Fig. 21.1 My page on Facebook. Room for one more...

One huge advantage is that I can now see exactly who my users are.

That's a mammoth change!

Until social media sites started popping up, users were just a list of IP addresses in the site logs. We might have known there were real people behind those numbers but we didn't know who they were, what they were interested in or what they were looking for.

The only time we came close to answering those questions was by attending conferences but even there, we only met the most dedicated readers.

Now though I can browse my list of friends on Facebook and see them face-to-face. I can see what they look like, I can see what they're working on and in the Facebook groups, I can chat with all of them at once about the projects I'm developing, answer their questions and discuss how I can better help them achieve their goals.

It's those groups that are really crucial.

They provide great forums for people with similar interests to come together and share information.

Facebook is a valuable tool for community-building but it has its limitations. It's really best at keeping friends and family in contact rather than users or customers... and you're not allowed to have more than 5,000 friends.

Your website will have more than 5,000 users so you can't have more than a fraction of them on your Facebook page at any one time. I used to send my extra applicants a thank you message and tell them that I'll add them as soon as space becomes available... until Facebook thought I was spamming and cancelled my account.

That could have been a disaster but it was actually a pretty good example of the power of Facebook.

Immediately afterwards, a group was formed on Facebook to urge the company to reinstate my account, and many of my 5,000 friends sent emails. Facebook agreed to give me my account back.

I don't send those emails any more but I am very aware of the influence that a loyal 5,000-strong community can have.

But it's Twitter that has proved to be much more effective at driving users to visit your site and take up your offers.

I love Twitter. I didn't expect to love Twitter but it's turned out to be so much fun and so effective that I haven't been able to stop using it.

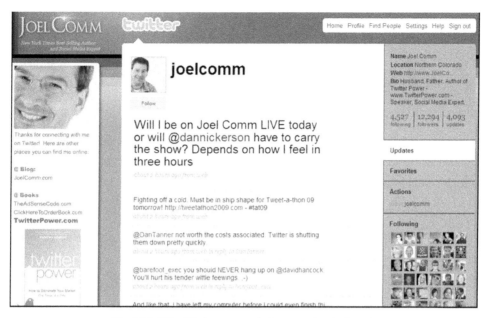

Fig. 21.2 I liked Twitter so much, I wrote a book about it.

The idea is very simple. You write a post — what Twitter calls a "tweet" — of no more than 140 characters that's supposed to describe what you're doing now. The tweet appears in your timeline and anyone can read it, reply to it and pass it on to their friends. Like Facebook, you can pick up friends, only Twitter calls them "followers," and more importantly, it doesn't limit the number so you can have tens and even hundreds of thousands of people following your tweets.

It sounds crazy. As a publisher you're going to beat your head against a wall to come up with something interesting to say in 350 to 500 words.

Now you have to do it in 140 *characters*, the maximum length of an SMS message. (Yes, you can also tweet from your mobile phone. One of the big advantages of Twitter is that you can use it anywhere.)

And yet, it's so easy. And so much fun. And so addictive.

Ever since I started tweeting, I haven't been able to stop. Of course, I don't just tweet about what I'm doing. I also use the service to chat with other Internet marketers, answer questions from users and readers, promote my books and seminars, ask for help when problems turn up (like the loss of my Facebook account), and to drive traffic to my website.

Clearly, that's always going to be useful. Write a new blog post and you can simply announce it in your timeline and place a link. That link has to be short though. A long, SEO-friendly title could take up a large chunk of the tweet and is bad etiquette.

You can use TinyURL at www.tinyurl.com to shorten the links but I found that service to be a little limiting. It was one thing to send people from Twitter to my account but I also wanted to keep track of the numbers clicking through.

Yes, even when using Twitter, it pays to be nuts about stats!

So we created TwitPwr.com, a URL-shortening service specifically for Twitter users.

Simply enter the URL of your new post, and you'll immediately receive a shorter version that you can cut and paste into your tweet. In addition though, you'll also be included on TwitPwr's site so that other users can see you, your tweets and your links.

It's a very neat way to help everyone to generate more traffic to — and through — their links.

Many bloggers use Twitter to do nothing more than announce their new content. That's fine as far as it goes, and you can even do it completely effortlessly. Twitterfeed, at www.twitterfeed.com, will turn your RSS feeds into tweets automatically.

Just upload your content and your subscribers will receive it — with an ad — in their RSS readers while your Twitter followers can see a notification, with a link, in their timelines.

... feed your blog to twitter

Getting started
Here's how to get your blog (or any other RSS or Atom feed) twittering:

1. **Create a new twitter user at twitter.com (or use your existing one)**

   this twitter user is going to be the one posting your blog entries - twitterfeed needs to know your chosen twitter username and password so it can post your blog updates to your twitter account

2. **Login to twitterfeed using your OpenID**

   OpenID is a standard for providing single sign on between web sites
   You can register your own OpenID for free, or may even be able to use your existing blog ID [more]

3. **Provide us with the URL for your blog's RSS feed, and how often we should post to twitter**

Fig. 21.3 Just tell www.twitterfeed.com where to find your
RSS feed and they'll tell your followers where to find you.

Darren Rowse, for example, does this to promote his Digital Photography School blog.

He's created a separate timeline specifically for the site that contains nothing but notifications created by Twitterfeed. When the timeline had 1,000 followers, Darren reported that each tweet was generating around 100 clickthroughs.

That's a 10 percent clickthrough rate for no effort whatsoever!

But Darren's site already has a large audience and Darren himself has a separate timeline in which he does a lot more than announce new content. He also discusses what he's doing, answers questions and makes the most of Twitter as a kind of open forum — the Internet's watercooler.

That's important. Twitter is a place in which people talk, connect, stay in touch and interact. It might have been designed as a place to make announcements but the public reply function and the ability to send confidential direct messages means that it's become a fantastic networking resource.

New from DPS: What Kind of Camera and Gear Should I Buy?: Today I want to post a question .. http://twurl.nl/2fkgnd

about 4 hours ago from twitterfeed

Fig. 21.4 This is the result of Twitterfeed in Darren Rowse's Digital Photography School timeline at www.twitter.com/digitalps.

If all you're doing is announcing your new content, you're not making the most of one of the Internet's most valuable tools.

There's about a zillion things you can do to build your followers and drive them to take the revenue-generating action that you want them to take. That's a subject for a whole other book, and you can read all about them in *Twitter Power*, my own guide to tweeting for profits.

To get started though, it's important to bear in mind these four strategies:

Link Facebook with Twitter

Facebook has its own in-house version of Twitter called "Status updates" but they're only seen by people on Facebook — a maximum of 5,000 friends.

Facebook's Twitter app though lets you place your tweets automatically on the site.

You can be sure you're reaching everyone and keeping your Facebook account dynamic and active for no extra effort.

Backgrounds Sell

Twitter only allows you to place one link on the bio. While you can also place links in your tweets, they move down the page as you reply to people and use the site.

The background however remains static.

Use the right-hand column to describe yourself and advertise your URLs.

Make Offers

Hard selling doesn't work on Twitter but you can reward your followers by supplying discount codes for following your tweets.

Dell is said to have generated more than a million dollars by placing its offers on Twitter. Whether you use the site to promote your own products or your affiliate products, Twitter provides a huge opportunity to turn your traffic into cash.

Get Help

And Twitter is also a huge knowledge resource. Ask a question on Twitter and you'll have a ton of answers in no time at all.

Getting stuck with your website design, your coding, an article idea or anything else no longer has to be a problem.

On Twitter, there's always someone available to lend a hand.

Few things have changed the Internet as dramatically as social media has done. While much of the praise has been overdone and overhyped, there's no question that I now consider it an essential part of my online marketing business and certainly the most enjoyable way to direct traffic to my ads and my offers.

You should too. For more on Twitter, you may want to pick up a copy of the book Twitter Power: How to Dominate Your Market One Tweet at a Time.

22. SEARCH ENGINE OPTIMIZATION

In the previous chapter, I talked about a number of different ways that you can increase your traffic. Probably the most important method though is to get a high ranking on search engines. That's free traffic.

Again, there are all sorts of books and experts who can help you improve your SEO and win a top spot for a site. These though are the strategies that have worked for me.

22.1 Robot.txt

The first thing you need to know about indexing your site at search engines is that you control which pages are indexed and which are excluded. You do that with a file called robots.txt.

Robots.txt contains nothing more than a record of which robots should index which pages.

Without going into too much detail, there are two conventions used in a robots.txt file:

User-agent: [Defines which robots the site is addressing.]
Disallow: [Allows you to list the sites or robots you want to exclude.]

In general, you're probably going to use "User-agent: *" to make sure that you're addressing the robots of every search engine and you'll probably want include all of your pages (although you might want to exclude your directories: "Disallow: /cgi-bin/").

Robots.txt just allows you to control which robots index which pages. It's important to have in your directory but it won't really increase your search engine rankings.

Titles, URL's and links are much more important.

22.2 Titles And URLs

I mentioned earlier that metatags just aren't what they used to be. I also said that it's important that your titles and URLs contain the most important keywords for each of your pages in order to keep the ads relevant.

But those titles and URLs don't just influence your ads; they also affect your search engine rankings.

A page about toy cars called cars.html might have a low ranking when someone looks for information about cars. Change the name to toy_cars.html and you should get a much higher ranking when someone looks for "toy cars".

The more relevant your URL is and the easier it is to read, the better. www.domain.com/page is always an improvement than http://domain.com/page.php?newsid=1234583373. That's why on my website www.familyfirst.com, I use URL's like www.familyfirst.com/miss_abigails_time_warp.html rather than strings of number which confuse the robots.

One of the first places you should look when you want to improve your rankings then is your titles and URLs.

22.3 Links

The more links you have, the better. And the better the sites that list those links the more they'll be worth. It is always worth aiming to put your links on sites that look good and have high rankings. In fact, being listed on a poor site can bring your ranking down.

One of the best places to place links to improve your search engine rankings is on forums. This isn't an exchange; you post your links on their site, they don't post their links on yours.

Make sure you browse forums regularly, add comments and include your URL in your signature. You're likely to get the best results on good forums related to your topic but don't be fussy. Even unrelated forums can help to improve your search engine ranking.

Google's spiders love forums and review them every week. And because these sites tend have quite high ranking, those posts will do wonders for your listings.

Of course, you shouldn't ignore the SEO forums themselves for some good tips. www.searchengineforums. com is one good place to browse and forums.seochat.com is another. You should also check out my own forum www.AdSenseChat.com. Although this is mostly about AdSense optimization, not surprisingly, SEO issues are discussed often, especially as they relate to AdSense. It's a great source to dig up new ideas.

And if you're going to be putting your links all over the forums, why not do the same thing for blogs?

You can think of blogs as places to read someone's writings if you like, but don't forget they also let you add your own feedback. That means that as an AdSense publisher, you should be thinking of them as free places to post your links. Again, any blog is good but top blogs on your topic are probably the best.

Don't forget to check out the SEO blogs too. www.seobook.com is a good one, www.bradfallon.com is another and of course there's my own blog at www.joelcomm.com. You're welcome to leave your links there!

It's not just blogs and forum that that let you leave your details though. There **are plenty of sites that welcome free content and would be happy to display your link** if it means that they get an article in return. Start by looking at other sites on your topic and then try www.ezinearticles.com. You don't even need to write anything original when you do this. If you write a new entry to your blog, submit it to an article site at the same time as you upload it to your blog. Who knows where your links will end up?

The easiest way to put your links across the Web though is to do a link exchange. **If you've got friends who have websites, start there.** That's very easy.

While linking from friends' sites is straightforward and cost-free, www.linkmetro.com makes the whole **link exchange** process very formal. There's a giant range of different sites that you can exchange links with so you can keep your links relevant and your ranking good and high.

You can also buy links on sites like www.AdBrite.com, and www.LinkAdage.com. Again, these allow you to choose sites on which you can place your own links but charge a fee for the process.

On my own site www.buyjoeldessert.com, for example, I give page links to people who satisfy my sweet tooth with a donation to my cause. (I'm still hungry by the way, so feel free to sign up, improve your rankings and make my dentist happy!)

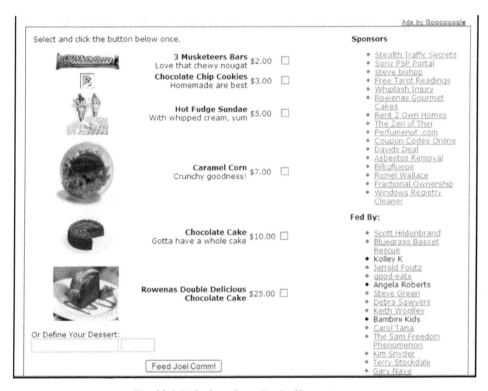

Fig. 22.1 Links for sale on BuyJoelDessert.com.

I know of several associates who have done something similar, allowing their visitors a tangible way to say "thank you" for their online efforts. Smart site owners see opportunity in this strategy as you can acquire quality links rather inexpensively. Here are some additional examples:

www.buyleoalatte.com
www.buybarbaracoffee.com

And finally, one resource that I highly recommend is **WebRing** (www.webring.com). This is such an easy way to gather links on relevant sites that I can't believe it's not the talk of the net.

The idea is to link together sites on similar topics so that users can quickly find topics that they're interested in. Nice for them. But it's nicer for you when a bunch of links from similar sites rocket your SEO ranking. That's exactly what Google and other search engines are looking for when they rank sites.

That makes WebRing a hugely powerful tool.

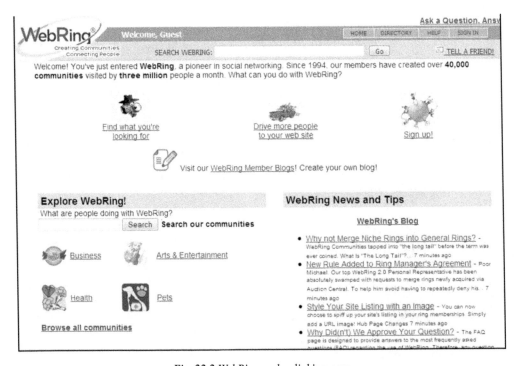

Fig. 22.2 WebRing makes linking easy

22.4 Create Gateways

Usually, your links will lead directly to your home page. That's where you see your site as starting and that's where you want them to enter.

But if the content the user wants to see is on one of the internal pages, there's no reason for them to have to click around to find it. Fill that page with keywords that relate to the content on that page and it will have its own search engine ranking — and well-targeted ads.

So if you have a site about cats and one of your pages was about cat food, it would make sense to put plenty of cat food keywords on the page. That would get you cat food ads and a high ranking on search engines when someone does a search for "cat food" rather than just people who wanted to know about "cats."

22.5 Automatic Submissions

Submitting your site to all of the search engines from Google and Yahoo! right down to the smallest ones, and optimizing each of your pages for high ranking can be a drag. You also have to keep submitting the site on a regular basis and constantly check your position if you want to keep it.

The search engines are always re-indexing and reorganizing. A site that can be in the top spot one week can be a couple of pages over a week later. (Good news if you're low down, not so good if you've spent hours changing your pages to climb the rankings.)

That's why many webmasters simply outsource their SEO so that they can concentrate on content.

There are lots of companies that do this. Search Engine Blaster (www.searchengineblaster.com) for example, lets you choose from over 600,000 engines but there are plenty of others.

Personally, I think that's a bit of a waste of time. Only Google, Yahoo and MSN are important, in that order.

22.6 SEO Tools

There are a number of tools that I recommend to help with search engine optimization. The first is the Google Toolbar, which will let you keep track of your page ranking. You can download it for free at toolbar.google.com.

Fig. 22.3 The Google Toolbar: Pretty and useful too.

The Alexa toolbar is also useful and will show you how your site ranks against others. You can download the Alexa toolbar at www.alexa.com/site/download.

Fig. 22.4 The Alexa Toolbar: Is your site number one yet?

22.7 A Word About Cloaking

One issue that surfaced recently in the contextualized advertising world is "cloaking": presenting a different site to the Google bot than the one you present to users.

There can be good reasons for doing this. If you've got a forum for example, the bot could read all the information on your page related to forums, links and the design etc., find that it outweighs your forum content and serve you ads related to forums in general instead of your site in particular.

You could also find that your search engine listings are affected too: instead of appearing nice and high on the results page following a search for your topic, you might only appear to people looking for forums. That's not likely to win you much traffic.

One solution is to strip the site down using javascript or one of the tools available online so that when the Google bot comes, it only reads the content.

Of course, you could also fool the bot into thinking that your site is about... well, anything really. You could spam Google into showing your site to anyone who was searching for anything.

And that's why Google banned the practice altogether.

Any form of cloaking, whether it's to get better targeted ads, improve your search engine rankings... or spam the search engines is a breach of Google's TOS and could get you banned.

So what should you do if you find that your design has a bigger influence on your ads and ranking than your content?

The best — and simplest thing to do — is to make sure that the description and keyword metatags are all filled in properly with terms relevant to your content.

Section Targeting can de-emphasize problematic areas of your website and might well affect your search engine rankings (it's certainly worth a try).

And if these don't solve your problem, you might want to think of a redesign.

22.8 TrafficAndConversion.com

I said at the beginning of this chapter that this book is about AdSense and not about SEO rankings. That's because I know much more about AdSense than I do about search engine optimization.

We all have our strong points and AdSense is mine.

If you're looking for someone whose strong point is search engine optimization though, I recommend Mark Widawer at www.trafficandconversion.com.

Many of the ideas in this chapter came as a result of me raiding his brain for some great strategies. If you're looking for more of the same, you should definitely check out his site and see what he has to say.

You won't regret it.

Part 5

Quick Tips

23. ADSENSE PROHIBITIONS, MISTAKES AND PROBLEMS

Google is very protective of its AdSense program and is a pretty strict ad provider. It has a relatively long page of Terms and Conditions (www.google.com/adsense/terms) and monitors sites pretty closely. While YPN usually sends a warning to sites that it believes have broken its terms and conditions, Google has been known to cut people off right away.

And that can be pretty painful.

I do recommend that you read the AdSense Terms and Conditions. I realize that they're not much fun and they're hardly a gripping read but they are important, especially when you start really pushing your ads to their limits. To make it easier for you though, I've gone through those terms and pulled out the most important restrictions contained in them.

This list is not a replacement for reading the Terms page — you're still going to have to do that. They just might make it clearer so that you're less likely to make a very costly mistake.

- **One individual or entity cannot hold more than one AdSense account; all accounts will be closed.**
  This is important if you have many sites covering different topics and are worried about the effects of Smart Pricing. You might want to open a separate account in a different name or open more than one business. Don't do it.
- **You cannot modify the JavaScript or other code provided in any way.**
  Google is pretty strict about this. Cut into the code and you risk the axe.
- **Web pages cannot contain solely ads, a Search Box or a referral button.**
  Blank pages with nothing more than AdSense ads are pretty rare; pages which contain only ads of different types are much more common. Google is working against these sorts of things and you'll probably find yourself if not banned, then almost certainly Smart Priced out. The only exception to this is AdSense for Domains but they can have nothing but AdSense for Domains.
- **Ads cannot appear on pages that are used for registration, chat, contain adult, objectionable or illegal content. And they can't be used in emails either.**
  If you have a site that's in any way morally objectionable, then AdSense isn't for you. That's the bottom line.

More relevant for most people though is the idea that you can't put AdSense on every page of a website. There are all sorts of pages on many people's sites that really don't contain any content, like password pages or error messages. You can't use them as places to put ads.

- **You cannot generate searches, clicks or impressions by any method other than genuine user interest.**
  So no automatic bots or clicking your own ads or any of that nonsense. That's just fraud and Google will spot it in a second.

- **You cannot display anything on your Web page that could be confused as an AdSense ad.**
  That's an interesting rule that prevents people from putting up affiliate links that look like ad units to try to cash in on Google's brand. In theory, this rule could cause a problem for someone who blended the ads into the page by making link lists that looked similar to ad units. As long as those links aren't ads though, and as long as you don't write "Ads by Goooogle" on them, I doubt if Google would have a problem with them.

- **You cannot put related images right next to an AdSense unit.**
  The old strategy of using images related to the ads to draw eyes to ad units has gone. Google doesn't want any pictures next to an ad unit so that they look like they're part of the ad. There's no clear definition of how far the images should be or how it defines 'confusing.' The best bet is to use common sense. If you're going to put an image near an ad unit, make it a logo, unrelated to the content of the ad unit or some part of the site.

- **If you're using a Google Search box, you cannot use any other search service on the page.**
  Again, Google wants a monopoly of services on your site. You can't offer your users the option of searching through Google or Yahoo; it's either-or, not both-and.

- **You cannot put anything between the ad link and the ad site.**
  So if you were thinking of trying to capture your lost traffic by redirecting ad clicks to another of your sites, think again. But who thinks of that?

- **You cannot communicate to advertisers directly concerning the ads on your site.**
  That would have been quite useful. You could have written to an advertiser and suggested ways in which they could make their copy more effective for your users.
  Of course, you could also suggest they advertise directly on your site and cut out the Google middleman...

- **You cannot change the order of the information in an ad unit.**

  This is pretty well covered by the ban on changing the code. But again, it might have been nice to put the ads that are most likely to get the most clicks at the top of the list, even if they pay less. But putting the ones with the highest bid price there isn't a bad idea either.

- **You cannot reveal your clickthrough rates or any other information about your site performance.**

Which is why I haven't quoted my own CTR figures in this book. But you can reveal the amount of Google's gross payments to you, which I have done.

These rules are all pretty straightforward and for the most part, easy to follow. Usually, if someone has been banned from AdSense it's because they've clicked on their own ads and Google didn't believe that it was an accident. That's just rotten luck.

23.1 The Difference Between Invalid Clicks and Fraudulent Clicks

Or rather, it's rotten luck unless it's outright fraud.

Check your stats and you might notice that there's a difference between the number of clicks you've received and the number of clicks that Google is prepared to pay you for.

That's because Google will have decided that some of those clicks are "invalid."

Google doesn't explain in detail what exactly an invalid click might be. It could be something as simple as the second of a user's double-click on an ad link but it could also be as horrible as automated clicks generated by a program.

Those aren't just "invalid clicks," they're also fraudulent clicks.

And the results can vary too. If you're lucky and it's clear that the invalid click was generated accidentally, Google simply won't credit your account.

If you're not lucky, Google will simply cancel your account.

23.2 The Biggest Mistakes That AdSense Publishers Make... And How To Avoid Them

Clicking on your own ads and finding your account canceled isn't the only bad luck AdSense publishers have run into. There are lots of different ways that you can make a mistake when using AdSense and while some of them Google will be pretty quick to tell you about, others you'll only feel in your pocket.

Here are some of the biggest mistakes you can make when using AdSense. Be aware of them... and beware of them!

Big Mistake #1: Not Being Familiar With Google's TOS

On the one hand, this is an easy mistake to make. The terms of service change all the time and what's legal one day could be illegal the next — and you could know nothing about the change.

On the other hand though, if something you've been doing is suddenly made illegal you probably shouldn't be doing it anyway.

The bottom line is to check the TOS regularly and to make a habit of browsing the AdSense forums. Even if you miss a change, it's unlikely that other people will.

It's a mistake not to stay informed.

Big Mistake #2: Inviting Others To Click Ads

That clicking your own ads is a mistake is pretty clear. There's no reason to do it and no excuse for doing it.

That also includes asking other people to click on the ads for you.

For site owners used to asking their users to support their sponsors, this can take some getting used to. Once the ads are up and optimized, there's nothing more that you can do to persuade people to click.

If you've got a line on your website that asks people to support your sponsors or if you've been asking people to click on your ads in any sort of way, you're making a giant mistake.

That's the sort of mistake that can get you banned.

Big Mistake #3: Using The Wrong Ad Blocks

Those first two mistakes will get you banned. The remaining mistakes will "only" cost you money.

Choosing the wrong ad blocks is one of the easiest mistakes to make. Almost any block can fit in almost any space but only one block will give you the highest revenues possible.

Use this book as a guide to which blocks suit which locations best and check out the case studies to see how other people are using a similar spot. Even if you're happy with your results so far, it's always possible that you could do even better.

Sitting on your laurels with the wrong ad block is certainly a mistake.

Big Mistake #4: Using The Wrong Colors

Exactly the same is true of your choice of colors. Forget about looking for some nice contrast or coming up with some snazzy design, you want the colors in your ads to match the colors on your site.

The background color should be the same as the background of your site and the font colors should match too.

Any other color is usually a mistake.

Big Mistake #5: Poor Page Placement

Some places on your page are much more powerful than others. You want to put your ads where your users are going to be looking, not where they'll make the page look good.

That might be at the beginning of an article, in the sidebar, at the top of the page, next to an image or any one of several dozen other spots.

Don't be shy about putting your ads front and forward. As long as they're blended into the site, they won't be anything like as obtrusive as you think. They'll be right in front of your users and attractive enough to click.

Big Mistake #6: Not Using AdLink Units

A common mistake that people make when they first start using AdSense is to assume that only the ad units are worth taking.

That's a big mistake.

Clicks on AdLink units make up a serious part of my AdSense earnings. When used properly, they should be a serious part of your AdSense earnings too. Don't overlook AdLink units just because they're small. Put them in the right place and you'll find that they can be very, very powerful

Big Mistake #7: Not Checking And Analyzing Stats

One of the biggest differences between AdSense publishers who get the big checks and AdSense publishers who earn pennies is that the big earners are addicted to reading their stats — and they understand what they're reading.

It's very tempting once you've set up your site and put on your ads to just kick back and look at the bottom line. But the other lines tell you what's working and what you should be doing.

Read your stats carefully and regularly.

Big Mistake #8: Ignoring Channels

If you're not sure how to use channels, don't let it ride. Read the chapter on channels again, build some and play with them.

For some people channels can look a little scary. You have to build them from scratch, you might not be too sure which channels you should create or what you should do with the data the channels should give you.

None of those is a good excuse. Channels are easy to build and they give you heaps of information about the way each of your Web pages is operating that you just couldn't get anywhere else.

If you're not using channels, you need to start.

Big Mistake #9: Not Keeping An AdSense Journal

When you were at school and your English teacher told you to keep a journal, you probably groaned, ignored her... and made up a month's worth of entries the day before you were supposed to bring it in to class.

When you're trying to make a lot of money with AdSense, keeping a journal is vital. It's the only way to keep track of your changes and what happened when you implemented those changes.

Every time you use a different ad block, push a different keyword or try a new location on the page, write it down, wait a week and write down the effect. If you're doing the same thing time and time again because you forgot what happened when you did it last time, you're wasting your time and your money.

Big Mistake #10: Building Huge Sites Overnight

It's possible to go from no site to AdSense site in just a few minutes (plus the time it takes to get the confirmation letter). But it will take a little while longer to build the sort of massive site that keeps users coming back and builds a loyal base.

Sure, you can use free books to fill dozens of pages and you can use already prepared content, but neither of these methods are as good as creating a huge site filled with original material.

That takes time.

Rush it and it's more likely you'll end up with a lot of trash that kills your clicks and ruins your Smart Pricing than a quality site that makes you money. It's better to be small and good than big and bad.

Big Mistake #11: Building Throwaway Sites

And if it's a bad idea to build large trashy sites, it's a terrible idea to build small, trashy sites.

Check out the AdSense forums long enough and there's a good chance that you'll come across plenty of publishers who believe not in creating good quality sites but in building small garbage-y ones and trying to squeeze as much revenue out of them as possible.

The advantage is that you can throw up a lot of them in a small amount of time and for little cost.

The disadvantage is that the returns are small too — and most important, they're just no fun to do.

I thoroughly enjoy managing every one of the sites I've created. It's because I enjoy them that my users enjoy them. That keeps them coming back and it keeps them clicking. And it keeps me coming back too.

If you're building throwaway sites just to make a quick buck, you're working too hard... and that's a giant mistake.

Big Mistake #12: Doing AdSense Halfway

This was the big mistake that I made for a long time. It's also the big mistake that about 95 percent of AdSense publishers are making.

They create their site, put up an AdSense unit, maybe they'll optimize it a little (and maybe not), and then they'll wait for the checks to come in.

Making a lot of money with AdSense will take a lot of work. It can make you more money than most people will make in most full-time jobs but it's not the sort of thing you can throw up in a morning and then spend the afternoon shopping for your beach house in Cancun.

You can start earning in the morning. But if you want to make real money, you're going to have to go all the way.

Anything less is a big mistake.

Big Mistake #13: Only Using AdSense

Don't get me wrong, I still think that AdSense is the greatest way to earn money from a website short of buying Google. But ever since Google changed its TOS to allow other kinds of advertising systems on AdSense pages — even other kinds of contextualized advertising systems — I've been happily mixing, matching and earning even more.

You should certainly use one of the text link services like Kontera. You can use Chitika if you have a good product-related site. You can recommend affiliate products. You can mix different payment systems so that your pages are earning by impression, by click and by sale.

You should have every base covered and every income stream up and running.

23.3 What To Do If Your AdSense Account Gets Closed

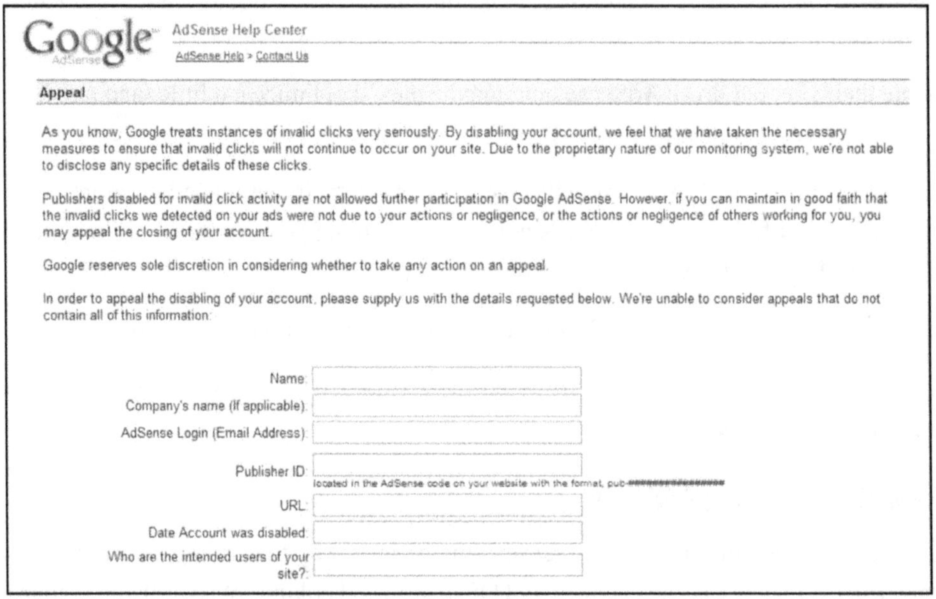
Google AdSense

AdSense Help Center

AdSense Help > Contact Us

Appeal

As you know, Google treats instances of invalid clicks very seriously. By disabling your account, we feel that we have taken the necessary measures to ensure that invalid clicks will not continue to occur on your site. Due to the proprietary nature of our monitoring system, we're not able to disclose any specific details of these clicks.

Publishers disabled for invalid click activity are not allowed further participation in Google AdSense. However, if you can maintain in good faith that the invalid clicks we detected on your ads were not due to your actions or negligence, or the actions or negligence of others working for you, you may appeal the closing of your account.

Google reserves sole discretion in considering whether to take any action on an appeal.

In order to appeal the disabling of your account, please supply us with the details requested below. We're unable to consider appeals that do not contain all of this information:

Name:

Company's name (If applicable):

AdSense Login (Email Address):

Publisher ID:

located in the AdSense code on your website with the format, pub-################

URL:

Date Account was disabled:

Who are the intended users of your site?:

Fig. 23.1 Google's court of appeal. You don't want to come here.

Most of the mistake people make at AdSense hit them in the wallet. Some mistakes though can hit where it really hurts and get your account closed. So what should you do if you get that dreaded email from AdSense informing you that your account has been shut down?

Well, the first thing to remember is that you've pretty much got no power at all. Google's Terms make it very clear that they have the right to kick someone out of their program whenever they feel like it and you have to prove your innocence.

But the people at Google aren't a nasty bunch and they will listen to you if you feel you've been hard done by. Your first step then should be to send them an email asking why you've been banned.

The most likely reason will be invalid clicks.

That might not mean that you've accidentally clicked your own ads. Google accepts that accidents do happen and takes occasional clicks like these into account. They'll show up as clicks in your stats but you won't earn revenue from them. Nor do you need to inform them every time your cursor accidentally lands on one of your ads.

But if it's more than occasional, you could be in trouble. It's possible that someone else might have been clicking ads on your site repeatedly — perhaps a competitor hoping to hit your earnings or a family member who didn't know it was forbidden.

It's also possible that someone has stolen your AdSense code and placed it on their own site. It sounds strange, but publishers have been concerned about this so Google now lets you create a list of Allowed Sites. Only those clicks on those sites will count towards your income.

And at least one publisher has been banned because the previous owner of the domain had clicked his own ads before the domain was sold.

Whatever the reason, the next step is to appeal. Google has an official appeal form. It's available at www.google.com/adsense/support/bin/request.py?contact=invalid_clicks_appeal.

Be sure to fill in all the fields in the form and provide as much information as possible.

Be polite. Remember, Google's system has detected a strange pattern in your click rate and is acting to protect its advertisers from paying for nothing. When advertisers start to feel that Google isn't looking after their budget, none of us will make money. If Google has made a mistake, you want to help the company correct it, not annoy it so much it won't want you back.

Someone will read your form, and you want to stay on that person's good side.

Provide proof of your innocence if you can and show that you're genuinely trying to help them get to the bottom of the problem. If you spotted a click spike in your stats, tell them when you saw it and what you think might have caused it — if you have any suspicions. If you happen to know the IP address of the source of the multiple clicks, block it, supply it to Google and tell them you've blocked it.

And remind Google that you think its service is great and that you'd like to keep using it.

There are plenty of stories around about publishers who got banned but were reinstated after appeal. If you can produce a good explanation of the events that led to your site being banned, there's a good chance that you'll be allowed back in.

And if all else fails and you find yourself cut off, there's always Yahoo! Publisher Network combined with Chitika and Kontera ads.

It's unlikely you'll make as much as you did with AdSense, but you will still make something.

24. TROUBLESHOOTING — WHAT TO DO IF YOU'RE NOT GETTING THE RESULTS YOU WANT

Follow the advice and strategies I lay out in this book and you should find that you get the results you want: a big fat check every month from the nice people at Google.

But it doesn't always work out that way. There will be times when you'll be scratching your head and wondering why things just aren't going the way you'd like them to. When that happens, check out the list of problems here and see if you can find a solution.

And if you can't find a solution here, check out AdSenseChat.com. Whatever I've missed here, you should be able to find there.

24.1 Low Revenues

This is the bottom of line of AdSense advertising and if your revenues are low then it couldn't be clearer that you're doing something wrong.

Unfortunately, it's going to take a bit of work to make clear what exactly it is that you're doing wrong.

If your revenues are much lower than you'd like then there are a number of different possible reasons and you need to check each of the following in turn:

- **Your traffic levels.** If you don't have the traffic, you won't get the revenues. A low level of traffic could be one reason why you're only making a low level of income.
- **Your CTR.** Increasing your traffic might not raise your income as much as you want if your clickthrough rate isn't all it should be. Once you've checked your traffic levels, take a look at how much of that traffic you're converting into clicks.
- **Your click price.** When the ads change all the time it's not always easy to figure out how much each click is worth but if you divide your daily income by your daily clicks you can get an idea of how much you're earning per click. If that figure is hovering around five cents, you're not making much — and you need to be making more.

You won't be able to make a move until you've figured out which of these potential problems is yours, and it's likely that your problem will be a mixture of more than one of them.

Your first move then, when you're not making the money you'd like, is to check each of these possibilities. Your next move is to solve the problem you've found.

24.2 Low Traffic Levels

If your problem is that your site isn't getting the traffic it needs, there are a whole range of different options you can take. I've covered the basic ideas in chapter 21 — and you can take another look to see if there's anything you've missed — but you also might want to try one of the courses or books that specialize in generating traffic.

It might cost you a few bucks but when it comes to making money with AdSense just about any investment is worth the effort. You should be able to make it back in no time.

24.3 Low Clickthrough Rates

When your clickthrough rates are very low, you're really in AdSense territory. This is all about getting the right ads in the right places. There all sorts of possible strategies that you can do and again, you're going to have to check each one in turn.

- **Are you using the right ad units?**
  Compare your site to the case studies in this book, to other sites on the Web and to the recommendations I make about where to put each of the different kinds of ad units. Those examples and recommendations should be your starting point.
  If they don't work for you though, you're going to need to do some experimenting. This can take a bit of time, but it's well worth the effort. Try replacing an ad unit with one of a different size and follow the stats. If they improve, you're on the right track.
- **Are you using the right colors and font?**
  This is a very easy one to fix. If the colors of your ads don't match the colors on your site, change them.
- **Are there better places on the page to put your ads?**
  Even if you're getting the right ads and they're well-blended, if no one sees them, no one will click them. Check to make sure your ads are in the most prominent positions. If you think you might do better if they were in different spots, move them and follow the results.

24.4 Low Click Price

Raising your click price is one of the trickiest challenges in AdSense. Because Google decides how much to charge advertisers for a click on your site, you can only affect their decision indirectly. Again there are a few things that you can do:

1. **Target different keywords**

   Different keywords pay different amounts. It's possible that your site is bringing up the lowest paying terms in your subject. Browse keyword sites to see what people are paying for words in your field and try creating a page that focuses on the highest paying term.

   If that page brings in good revenues, you've got a keyword problem — and that's easy to fix. If you're still getting a low click price, you've got a low Smart Price rating, and that's going to take a bit more work to fix.

2. **Buy better traffic**

   Your Smart Price suffers when your users click but don't buy. One solution is to buy better targeted traffic that's more likely to be interested in what your ads are offering. For example, you could try working backwards and target your traffic to the ads you're currently showing.

3. **Build better content**

   Or it could be that people are clicking your ads not because they're interested in them but because they're not interested in what's on the page. Good quality content will deliver high quality clicks from people who are motivated to buy from your advertisers.

   There are no shortcuts to building great content. You can try to focus on a topic that genuinely excites rather than building a site just for the money. You could try buying in some professionally written articles by taking a freelancer from eLance, and seeing if that raises your click price. Or you could just take another look at what your best competitors are doing — and do the same.

- **Remove poor-performing ads**

   Your Smart Price is affected by all the sites in your account. One poor-performing site then can bring down your prices across all your sites. If you own lots of different sites and your ads aren't getting the price you think they deserve, one strategy could be to remove the ads from the sites that you think aren't doing so well.

Whichever strategy you choose, the goal will be to get more of the users to click on the ads to buy from your advertisers. You should start to see a change in your price within a couple of weeks.

24.5 Low Ad Relevance

If your ads aren't relevant, people won't want to click them. Try Section Targeting to focus Google on the ideas you want to emphasize. (If that works you might want to take things a little further by turning each section into a different page. That will give even more ads and more opportunities to earn).

Alternatively, you can play with the keywords on your page, change the title of each page so that they include a keyword you're trying to target or include more section titles. All of these options should help to keep your ads on track.

It's also possible that at least part of your site requires users to log in. Google's AdSense Crawler can't do that so it can't tell Google which ads to serve on those membership pages. So you get irrelevant ads.

The solution is to use the Site Authentication link under your AdSense Setup tab. You'll have to confirm that the site is yours but once you've done that, it's just a question of providing the crawler with a username and password.

24.6 Too Many Public Service Ads

Public service ads are another sign of a keyword problem. You might not be hitting the keywords you want, or it could be that there simply aren't any ads for the keywords you're aiming for.

The first thing you need to do is make sure that you've got something to show instead of public service ads, nice though they are. Specify an alternate URL to make sure that you're still earning even when the keywords aren't working.

Your next step though, is going to be to fix the problem. Make sure that Google does have ads for the keyword you're targeting (you can use one of the preview tools such as googleadspreview.blogspot.com to do this). If nothing comes up, you'll need to throw different keywords onto your page.

If something does come up — and it's not what you're getting — you can just use all of the keyword strategies I mentioned earlier to dump those PSAs.

24.7 My Ads Have Disappeared!

When Google made it possible for publishers to name their ad units and change them all automatically without repasting the code, it wanted to make sure that publishers didn't accidentally delete them.

So Google didn't create a delete feature.

Instead ad units that aren't shown for seven days are automatically made inactive.

If your ads are on a page that gets no traffic at all — perhaps because it's a test page or because it's just been built — those ads might disappear. You'll need to make the ads active again... and look at them at least once a week until you show the page to users.

24.8 Too Few Ads In A Unit

Sometimes a four-ad ad unit will only show one or two ads. There's nothing you can do about this and it's not really a problem. If you're getting just one ad, you could be earning by CPM instead of cost-per-click. If you're getting two ads — as Google likes to serve them sometimes — you just have to hope that they're doing it because it pays better.

With AdSense, you don't get to control everything!

24.9 I'm Not Getting Any Ads At All

One problem that strikes some websites is that the space they've allotted for ad units remains empty. Instead of seeing ads alongside their content, they get... nothing at all.

And often, the problem — and the solution — is very simple.

It might be that there's a problem with the code. Paste the AdSense code in the wrong place in your HTML and you can give your website all sorts of problems. But usually, those problems won't be limited to a non-functioning AdSense unit. Your cells will be misplaced and the page won't look right.

You'll need to take out the AdSense code and try it again somewhere else on the page. It's all straightforward enough for this to be a rare problem.

More tricky is websites that require users to log in. Dating sites, for example, tend offer little to unregistered users beyond the ability to look at a few pages of search results, and forums keep all sorts of goodies back to tempt users to leave their registration details.

For Google, sites like these pose a problem. AdSense's crawlers can't get past the login pages, so they can't place ads on them.

Fortunately, there is a fairly simple way around this problem too. You'll need to create an authentication rule using the Site Authentication feature in your AdSense account. (You can find it under the AdSense Setup tab.) It's just a little bit complicated — you have to use Google's Webmaster tools then verify the site — but Google guides you neatly through the process.

The result should be that even those pages which lie behind a login page can still earn ad revenue.

24.10 I Still Need Help!

Making AdSense work really isn't difficult. Signing up is simple and so is pasting the code onto your pages so that they start to show ads.

The work comes in making the most of those ads and ensuring that you're monetizing as many of your users as possible.

But you could still run into problems. I've described the most common issues here, but if none of these describe a situation you've encountered, there are a few places you can look for help.

My own site AdSenseChat.com is one place. There are always interesting discussions going on there and plenty of people who are available to answer your questions. They include other users, as well as my own team members and I use the site myself sometimes too.

It's nice to be able to lend a hand directly.

Google though has its own resource at www.google.com/support/forum. This is a very active forum and while you'll probably find that there are more questions there than answers, it's not a bad place to look for a solution.

Even if no one provides you with a solution, searching old threads might turn up someone who asked a similar question. And looking through AdSense-related forums in this way can often throw up some interesting ideas and strategies that other people have been playing with.

A third place you can look for answers is Twitter.

Although I talked about Twitter as a place to drive traffic and sales, and build a closer link to your community of readers, it's a great place to meet other Internet entrepreneurs and ask advice.

Put up a question about AdSense in your timeline — or just ask someone directly — and there's a great chance that you'll get the answer you're looking for... and who knows, maybe some more traffic too.

25. STAYING UP TO DATE AND LEARNING THE LATEST ADSENSE TIPS

AdSense changes all the time and lots of people are following those changes. They're talking about what those changes mean for publishers and how you can take advantage of them.

They're also discussing the new contextualized advertising systems that appear from time to time and commenting on how well they work.

Most serious publishers pay close attention to these blogs and other sites. They're an invaluable source of first-hand information from people who have been there and done that. They'll save you a huge amount of time — and money.

I've put a short list of some of the most important sites to look at below. This isn't meant to be a complete list — that would be way too long — but these are a good place to start. They'll keep you in the loop and make sure your questions get answered.

- **www.JenSense.com**
  Jen's contextual advertising blog is a great read. She's always coming up with useful information and sometimes manages to dig up a real scoop (like what lies behind Smart Pricing). This should definitely be in your favorites.

- **www.ProBlogger.net**

  Darren is a blogger making a healthy six-figure income with his online thoughts and his advice about how to do the same thing. If you're running a blog, you really need to be reading it... and if you're not running a blog, you'll still find enough great advice to keep you busy too.

- **www.AssociatePrograms.com/discus/index.php**
  Forums are a really great place to swap ideas and most importantly, ask questions. Publishers who are old hands at making serious money with AdSense are usually more than happy to share their knowledge. The forum at Associate Programs is a great place to pick up tips about everything from links to marketing.

- **Forums.DigitalPoint.com**
  And the forums at Digital Point are at least as good, if not better, with plenty of information on AdSense.

26. CASE STUDIES

Throughout this book, I've been explaining all the different ways that you can optimize your site and boost your revenues. In this chapter, I've collected some examples.

All of these are real sites that employed the techniques that I describe in this book to make more money. I'll talk you through them so that you can see exactly what they did, why they did it — and how you can do the same.

26.1 JourneyAustralia.com — Unmissable Ads Down Under

Fig. 26.1 JourneyAustralia.com puts its ads front and center.

It can take some courage to make your ads the most important thing the user sees when he looks at the page, but that's the approach that JourneyAustralia.com takes.

You can't miss these ads! They're right above the fold and slap-bang in the middle. They're the first thing the reader sees even before he knows what the site is about.

Note too the picture right next to the ad unit. That helps to keep users' eyes in the ad zone, but you have to be very careful doing that. Google's ban on "misleading" images is vague enough for them to act on any picture placed next to an ad unit any time they want. That doesn't mean they will but you don't want to give them an opportunity. JourneyAustralia.com seems to have found the right sort of image to use. If you're not sure about your image though, it's best to leave it to one side.

The strategy of placing an ad unit in the middle of the page though is very simple. It's about as subtle as a slap in the face but it can be very, very effective.

Do you have the courage to try it?

26.2 Great Ideas For Integration From FreeAfterRebate.info

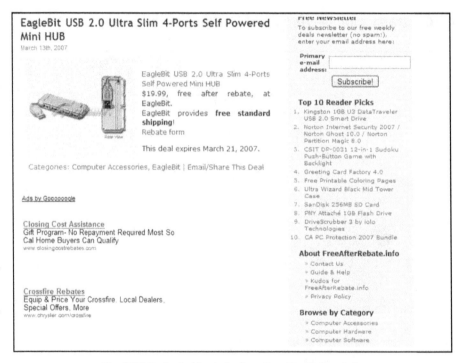

Fig. 26.2 Perfectly blended ads at FreeAfterRebate.info.

Few sites do a better job of integrating their ads with the text as FreeAfterRebate.info. The ad units have lost their borders, the text matches the text of the content and the background color is the same as the background color of the Web page.

The content itself is short as well. In fact, it looks a lot like an ad! That's a great strategy to use. Instead of blending an ad unit into a Web page, you can create content that matches the ad unit. I'm not sure whether this is what FreeAfterRebate.com did but there's no reason why you couldn't do it.

First, you'd decide on the format of your ad units, then you'd create very short articles that follow the appearance of those units. Because you wouldn't be able to include much more than a headline, a sentence or two of text and a link, you could really only use this strategy on pages that discuss products, or home pages that offer teasers to longer articles.

Look too though at the way this site uses an image. Instead of placing a picture right next to an ad unit, FreeAfterRebate.com puts it *above* the ad unit. That's another great solution to copy.

26.3 Gifts-911.com Gets Emergency Treatment With Multiple Ad Units

The most Adriana Copaceanu's site Gifts-911.com had made in one month was $31.19 — not much more than a dollar a day. She put a main ad unit above the fold, a second unit at the bottom of the page and an Ad Link unit on the right.

After making the ads more prominent and adding more of them, revenues doubled the following months and reached as high as $200 in the month after that!

That's was so simple. It's a great example of how just a small change in AdSense can yield massive results.

Could Adriana do more? Probably. But this is a pretty good start!

Check out Gift-911.com at www.Gifts-911.com.

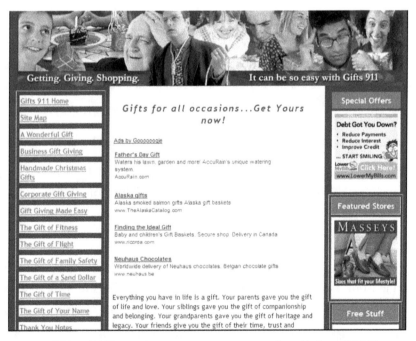

Fig. 26.3 Gift-911.com gives its own revenues some first aid above the fold...

26.4 OffshoreBankingCentral.com Brings Home The Bacon

One of the great things about optimizing your AdSense ads is that with a little bit of thought, you can really come up with some very clever ways of blending the ads into the page.

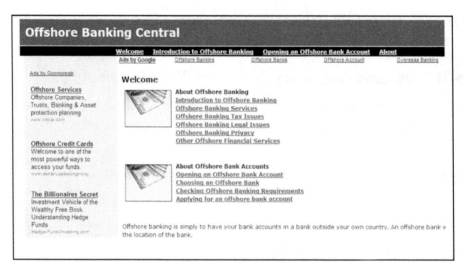

Fig. 26.4 A link unit disguised as a nav bar at OffshoreBankingCentral.com?

It's easier to do this with some ads than others.

Leaderboard text links, for example, can be very useful. A lot of people turn their nose up at horizontal text links. They think that because they're so small not enough people will see them to click on them. While vertical link units can be easily integrated into a list of links, there's no good place to put a horizontal unit.

That's a big mistake.

OffshoreBankingCentral.com shows just how powerful a well-blended horizontal link unit can be.

This site has two sets of ads: a vertical ad unit on the left separated from the rest of the page with a gray background (I'd be interested to know how well those ads perform but I suspect they'd do better with a white background); and a horizontal link unit at the top of the page.

That link unit just does an outstanding job.

The unit displays four links right beneath the navigation bar. Each one of those links contains either the word "offshore" or the word "banking." Even though "Ads by Google" is still there right next to those links, they still look like another line of navigation links leading to relevant parts of the site.

I think there's a very valuable lesson there about the value of link units.

While it's true that link units contain very little information, used correctly that can be an asset. Had there been another line or two describing the site those links lead to, it would have been clear that those links are ads. As it is, they're perfectly blended.

How can you copy what Offshore Banking Central did?

Easy. Create a very simple navigation bar made up of links rather than tabs and place your horizontal link unit directly beneath it. You'll need to make sure that you're hitting the keywords in just the way you want but if you pull it off, you should see some fantastic results.

26.5 Subtle Ad Linking At Sudoku Links

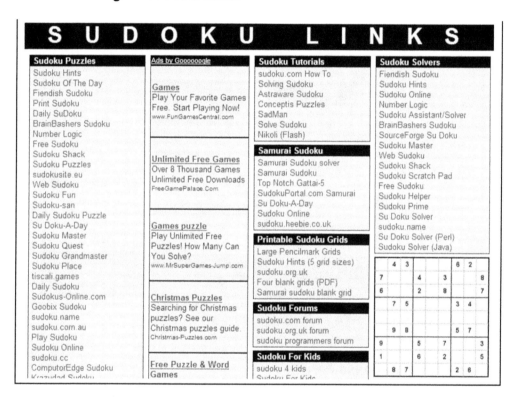

You have to look hard to spot the ads at SudokuLinks.com. The entire site consists of a series of vertical columns, filled with links. One of those columns is a vertical AdSense column which is placed in the middle of the page, not at the side where it would be ignored.

This is certainly a striking example of one way to blend an ad unit into a Web page but I doubt it's going to work for everyone. You might be able to follow this strategy on a Resources or Links page on your website but clearly the biggest problem is the lack of content.

The only content on the page consists of a small column right beneath the ad unit explaining how to play Sudoku.

That could be the sort of thing that drives down click value; Google prefers sites with lots of content rather than pages that contain nothing but links.

But you could still use this strategy on a site with dynamic content by, for example, placing teasers to articles in vertical or horizontal columns that match the AdSense unit. And you could make those content columns more obvious than pushing them to the bottom of the page.

In general though, this looks like an extremely effective strategy. If you can make it work for you, you should see some great results.

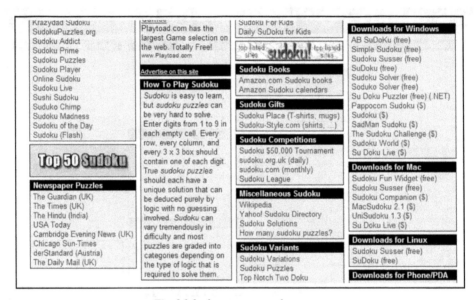

Fig. 26.6 ...but not too much content.

26.6 Go4th.org Takes AdSense Forward

Go4th.org also uses vertical columns, but this site has a much heavier focus on content and still manages to blend the ads in well. In fact, placing a vertical ad unit on the side of a blog has become pretty much a standard layout for many online publishers. You have a sidebar full of links, a link unit under the blog entry headline and a skyscraper on either the left or the right.

It's the obvious way to lay out a blog page, and it works.

But that doesn't mean you still can't be creative and come up with new ways to blend those ads into the page and make them more attractive to users.

Go4th.org does this in a really interesting way.

The blog entry — or rather, the articles that the site posts — are positioned in a wide space in the middle of the page sandwiched between two sidebars. The sidebar on the left is where the ads go. The sidebar on the right contain a bunch of links to external sites.

And this is where things get clever...

The design of each of those areas is exactly the same. Even the "Ads by Goooogle" line has been copied and turned into "May lead to external sites." That helps to draw the two parts together, an idea which is polished off by putting the word "More" above the ads and "Links" above the external links.

Those ads just don't look like ads any more; they look like the same sort of recommended links that are on the right hand side.

Fig. 26.7 More links... sorry ads, at Go4th.org.

This isn't the only place that the site blends ads well into the page. There's a second set of ads at the bottom of each article entry. What's nice about these ads is that they follow a little author bio that includes links itself. That helps users get used to reading content that contains links and might be ads.

Could the site get more clicks by replacing that banner ad unit with a square unit at the beginning of the article? Maybe. But that's exactly the sort of thing that can easily be tested.

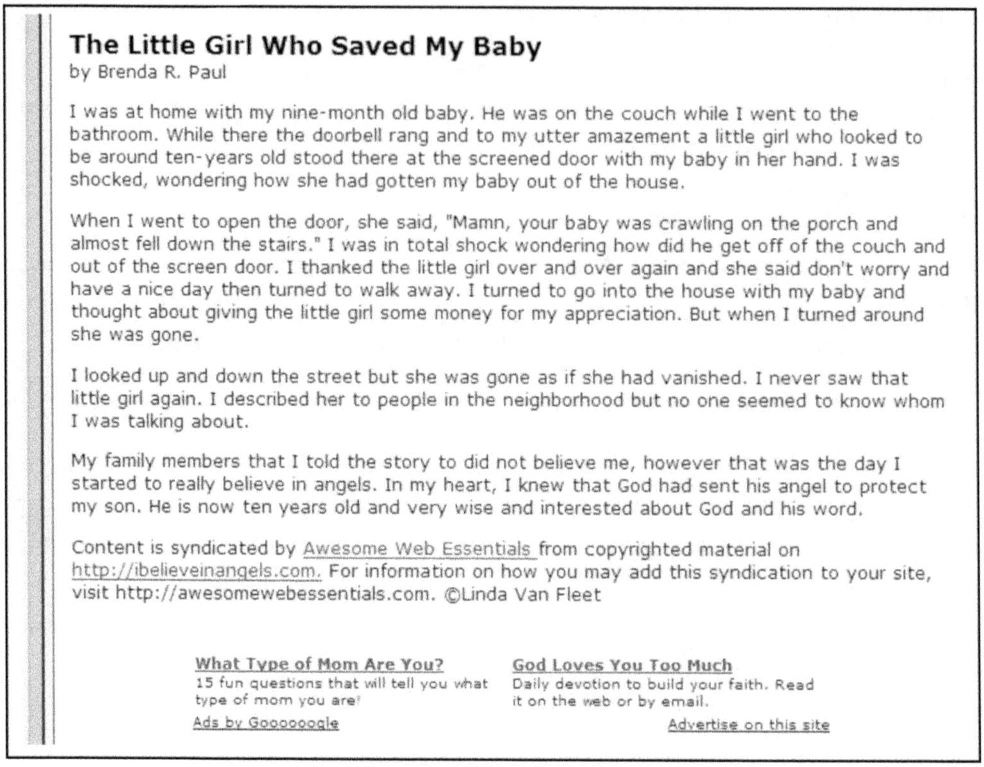

The Little Girl Who Saved My Baby
by Brenda R. Paul

I was at home with my nine-month old baby. He was on the couch while I went to the bathroom. While there the doorbell rang and to my utter amazement a little girl who looked to be around ten-years old stood there at the screened door with my baby in her hand. I was shocked, wondering how she had gotten my baby out of the house.

When I went to open the door, she said, "Mamn, your baby was crawling on the porch and almost fell down the stairs." I was in total shock wondering how did he get off of the couch and out of the screen door. I thanked the little girl over and over again and she said don't worry and have a nice day then turned to walk away. I turned to go into the house with my baby and thought about giving the little girl some money for my appreciation. But when I turned around she was gone.

I looked up and down the street but she was gone as if she had vanished. I never saw that little girl again. I described her to people in the neighborhood but no one seemed to know whom I was talking about.

My family members that I told the story to did not believe me, however that was the day I started to really believe in angels. In my heart, I knew that God had sent his angel to protect my son. He is now ten years old and very wise and interested about God and his word.

Content is syndicated by Awesome Web Essentials from copyrighted material on http://ibelieveinangels.com. For information on how you may add this syndication to your site, visit http://awesomewebessentials.com. ©Linda Van Fleet

What Type of Mom Are You?
15 fun questions that will tell you what type of mom you are!

God Loves You Too Much
Daily devotion to build your faith. Read it on the web or by email.

Ads by Goooooogle

Advertise on this site

Fig. 26.8 From bio to banner.

If you wanted to use a similar strategy on your site though, all you would need to do is put two sidebars on your site, make sure that they both look exactly the same but put ads in one and links in the other.

Easy!

26.7 Matching Articles To Ads... And Cell Phones

The usual way to blend ads into the site is to do 3-Way Matching: to make the ads match the rest of the site in terms of background color, font color and font.

It is possible to take a different approach though: you can make the site match the ads — or at least elements of it. Chris at GetACellPhone.com provides a fantastic example of this.

He's put one ad unit in the left-hand column but right above it and right below it, he's also put introductions to two articles. The headline of each article is a link to the rest of the piece further in the site and matches the headline of the ad.

That makes the ads look like links to articles, and it's a great idea.

As a strategy, it's very easy to copy, but I'd take it further. You can match the color of the URL under the ad to the color of the links on the rest of the page and restrict the size of the introduction to just two lines — just like the ads.

Make the rest of the page look like the ads and you'll do some great matching.

Fig. 26.9 Play "spot the ads" at GetACellPhone.com.

26.8 Brewing Up Profits With Herbal Tea

Some of the most effective optimization strategies are very simple. Some are very creative. At TeaHerbalTea.com, we get both types.

The site has three ad units above the fold: a banner ad immediately beneath the header; a horizontal text link above the content; and a large rectangle embedded in the content.

But look at how each of those units is blended into the site. The banner's background is lime-green, the same color as the site's background, the titles match the color of the site's header and the URL is kept just a tone or two above the background to make it almost invisible.

The unit embedded into the article follows a similar strategy. The title of the links match the title of the article, the description is kept black and the URL is a light color so that it almost disappears into the background.

It's in the text links though that things get really interesting. The site has been designed so that it looks like there are little tabs above each of the links. That's great idea. Would Google like it? It's hard to say. So far, it's not doing this site any harm, and it's not an image, but you might want to clear it with your friendly AdSense rep before you put in your site.

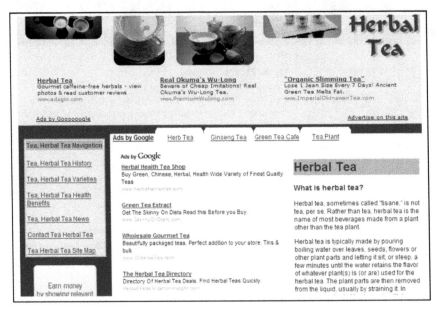

Fig. 26.10 Three superbly blended ads at TeaHerbaltea.com...

It's worth asking about.

The site's ads don't end there though. There's another ad unit below the fold in the middle of the page, a Google search box at the bottom of the page and even a couple of referral buttons and an Amazon ad on the left. And with that second square ad unit turning up such well-targeted ads, there's a great chance that they'll get clicked.

Organic Loose Green Tea
Rooibos, jasmine tea, oolong green tea, black tea
mysagebug.com

Varieties of Tea and Herbal Tea

There are numerous varieties of "real" teas and herbal teas. As mentioned previously, tea comes from the *Camellia sinensis* plant, while herbal teas are made with parts from other plants. Tea blends are usually made by mixing tea and other plants for a unique, flavorful brew. *More on varieties of tea and herbal tea >>*

Believed Health Benefits of Tea and Herbal Tea

Tea and herbal teas have historically been believed to have a wide variety of health benefits. Tea naturally contains caffeine, a known stimulant. Certain herbal teas have been said to calm down, or soothe, the person imbibing such teas. *More on the believed health benefits of tea and herbal tea >>*

Google [   ] [Search]

⊙ Web ○ www.teaherbaltea.com

Fig. 26.11 ...and rounding it all off with a search box.

26.9 Whispy Makes Ad Units Disappear!

Sometimes, you really don't have to do too much to get the sort of optimized ads that bring fantastic results. Whispy.com has done a great job of blending its ad links into its site.

First, it's used links in different colors. In general, that's not a good idea; your users expect links to be blue so that's the color you should make them — and the color you should make your ad links too.

But Whispy is only using two different kinds of blue: a bold blue which functions as the title for the profiles and link to the content; and a lighter blue for the links in the sidebars.

When the user sees ad links in exactly the same color, he'll just assume he's looking at more content links.

This is a very simple strategy that anyone can copy: just make sure that your ad links are the same color as the rest of your other links... and hide those ad links in a list of content links.

Very simple. Very, very effective.

Fig. 26.12 Just a perfect example of a camouflaged ad unit. How long did it take you to find it?

26.10 Mixing AdSense With Kontera On DealOfDay.com

Ever since Google changed its policy to allow publishers to combine different ad programs on the same page, finding ways to make the most out of multiple ad units has proved an exciting challenge.

I talked about how I blend horizontal ad units into my forum on DealOfDay.com but I've also been playing around with adding Kontera's ads on those pages too.

Earning revenue from forums isn't easy. I'm more likely to plan a forum as a way of supplying a service to my readers and building a community than as a way of earning income. People are just too focused on looking for answer to their questions to spend their time clicking ads. CPM ads often do better here.

But blending AdSense into the forum can work very well. And now I've found that adding link ads helps even more.

Notice how the two sets of ads look different and offer different things too. The AdSense ads look like category headings. In fact, this thread category was specifically about bargains on baby products, so I couldn't have asked for a better keyword there.

The Kontera ads though focus on specific products. That's their strength, and that's why it pays to use highly targeted terms when you're using Kontera (so "Tylenol" not "painkiller," "Playstation" not "video game system.").

The result on this forum was that I got to offer my readers a range of different types of ads... and picked up two different kinds of income.

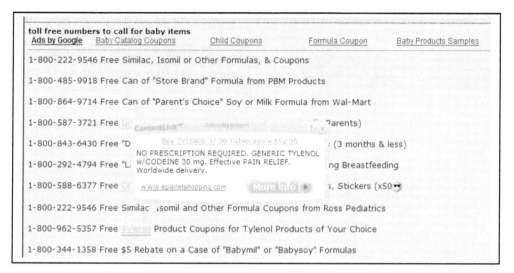

*Fig. 26.13 Increasing my earning potential by combining
ad systems on the DealOfDay.com forum.*

CONCLUSION

AdSense can give you huge amounts of money. It can pay your mortgage, make your car payments and send you on the sort of vacations you've only dreamed of. If you want, it can even let you give up the day job and look forward to a life of working at home, in your pajamas with no boss other than yourself.

Or it can give you enough money to buy a couple of candy bars each week.

The secret of AdSense success isn't complicated. You don't have to spend years in a classroom learning a new skill or head out to get a diploma. The principle is very basic:

Serve interesting ads to users in a way that makes them want to click.

You do that with layout. You do that by choosing the right size of ads. And you do it by blending the ad into the page.

Choosing the right keywords is important too, and so is bringing traffic to your site at a low price before selling them on to advertisers for a higher one.

Most important though is to keep a close eye on the results of everything you do so that you can see what works and what doesn't.

In this book, I've told you everything you need to know to supercharge your AdSense earnings. Apply the techniques I've described here, *track the results* and you should see your incomes rise as quickly as mine did!

May your AdSense revenue explode!

Joel Comm

GLOSSARY

The online advertising world uses all sorts of jargon to describe different bits of the process. If you're confused by a term, you should be able to find your answer here.

3-Way Matching — A method of blending ads into a Web page by matching the ad's background color, font color and font with the surrounding page content.

AdSense Code — The instructions to display ads on a Web page are contained within a piece of HTML code that is copied from Google's AdSense site. The code must be pasted onto each page on which you wish to display an ad.

Ad Rank — The order in which the ads appear in an ad unit is determined by Google. The ads at the top of the list should give you the most money based on cost-per-click and clickthrough rate.

Ad Unit — A group of ads displayed together as a set. You can display up to three ad units on one page, in addition to a search box and three link units.

Alternate Ads — Pre-determined ads that are served in place of public service ads when Google is unable to find contextual ads.

Channel — A method of tracking results across pages, sites, domains or any criteria set by a publisher.

Click — A click by a user on an ad. In stats reports, the clicks column may include invalid clicks but not clicks on public service ads.

Clickthrough Rate (CTR) — The number of clicks an ad receives divided by the number of impressions the ad receives. The higher your CTR, the better.

Contextual Advertising — Ads that are related to the content of the Web page on which they appear (as opposed to traditional banner ads that are served regardless of the content of the page).

Cost-Per-Click (CPC) — The amount an advertiser pays for each click his/her ad receives. AdSense uses a range of different types of Cost-Per-Click:

Maximum Cost-Per-Click — The maximum amount an advertiser is prepared to pay for each click.

Actual Cost-Per-Click — The amount an advertiser is charged for each click. The rate will vary according to the Smart Pricing rate of your site and the bidding price of competitors. Google always tries to charge advertisers the lowest rate possible.

Cost-Per-Thousand Impressions (CPM) — The amount an advertiser pays each one thousand times his/her ad is displayed. Like CPC, AdSense refers to different types of CPM:

Maximum Cost-Per-Thousand Impressions — The maximum amount an advertiser is charged for an impression.

Actual Cost-Per-Thousand Impressions — The amount an advertiser is charged for each impression. In general, this will be one cent more than the price required to keep the ad in its position on the page.

Effective Cost-Per-Thousand Impressions (eCPM)— The cost of one thousand ad impressions. Used by publishers to compare income rates across channels (and advertising programs). To calculate your eCPM, simply divide earnings by impressions (so $200 earned from 50,000 impressions would yield an eCPM of $4.00).

Filters — Used by publishers to block specific ads or groups of ads.

Google AdWords — Google's advertising program. Advertisers submit their ads to Google, specifying their maximum CPC and total advertising budget. The ads are distributed across AdSense publishers.

Impression — A single display of an ad somewhere on Google's ad network.

Page Impression — A single display of an ad on a publisher's Web page.

Pay-Per-Click — Often used interchangeable with Cost-Per-Click. Refers to a method of online advertising in which advertisers pay only when action is taken by the user and not only when an ad is served (CPM).

Placement Targeting — A strategy used by advertisers to choose the sites, locations and channels on which they would like their ads to run.

Public Service Ads (PSA) — Ads for non-profit organization that are served on Web pages when Google is unable to find relevant ads or cannot read the content on a Web page. Publishers are not paid for displaying public service ads.

Publisher — A member of AdSense whose sites display the AdSense code and Google's ads.

Search Engine Optimization (SEO) — A process of raising a site's rankings in the various search engines. This usually involves creating links from other sites, targeting keywords and building traffic.

Section Targeting — Lines of code used to focus Google's robots on specific, keyword-rich areas of a Web page.

Smart Pricing — A system used by Google to determine the value of the traffic sent by your site to advertisers and to price your ads accordingly. Sites that deliver high conversion rates to advertisers earn more than sites with low conversion rates.

BONUS

Instantly Download Two Chapters from Joel Comm's Best Selling Book *Twitter Power* for Free!

Twitter Power
How to Dominate
Your Market
One Tweet at a Time

Hello Friend,

Twitter is growing at an incredibly fast rate.

Businesses that are paying attention are finding social media to be a great way to connect with prospects and customers. But exactly how can Twitter be used to grow a business?

The answers are in my new book, Twitter Power.

Now, you can instantly download a free sample featuring two chapters from Twitter Power for free! Just go to this site:

http://twitterpower.com/free.

Joel Comm
New York Times Bestselling Author

BUY A SHARE OF THE FUTURE IN YOUR COMMUNITY

These certificates make great holiday, graduation and birthday gifts that can be personalized with the recipient's name. The cost of one S.H.A.R.E. or one square foot is $54.17. The personalized certificate is suitable for framing and will state the number of shares purchased and the amount of each share, as well as the recipient's name. The home that you participate in "building" will last for many years and will continue to grow in value.

THIS CERTIFIES THAT

YOUR NAME HERE

HAS INVESTED IN A HOME FOR A DESERVING FAMILY

1985-2005

TWENTY YEARS OF BUILDING FUTURES IN OUR
COMMUNITY ONE HOME AT A TIME

1200 SQUARE FOOT HOUSE @ $65,000 = $54.17 PER SQUARE FOOT
This certificate represents a tax deductible donation. It has no cash value.

Here is a sample SHARE certificate:

YES, I WOULD LIKE TO HELP!

I support the work that Habitat for Humanity does and I want to be part of the excitement! As a donor, I will receive periodic updates on your construction activities but, more importantly, I know my gift will help a family in our community realize the dream of homeownership. **I would like to SHARE in your efforts against substandard housing in my community!** *(Please print below)*

PLEASE SEND ME _____ SHARES at $54.17 EACH = $ $_____

In Honor Of: _____

Occasion: *(Circle One)*   HOLIDAY   BIRTHDAY   ANNIVERSARY

   OTHER: _____

Address of Recipient: _____

Gift From: _____   *Donor Address:* _____

Donor Email: _____

I AM ENCLOSING A CHECK FOR $ $_____ PAYABLE TO HABITAT FOR HUMANITY OR PLEASE CHARGE MY VISA OR MASTERCARD *(CIRCLE ONE)*

Card Number _____ Expiration Date: _____

Name as it appears on Credit Card _____ Charge Amount $ _____

Signature _____

Billing Address _____

Telephone # Day _____ Eve _____

PLEASE NOTE: Your contribution is tax-deductible to the fullest extent allowed by law.
Habitat for Humanity • P.O. Box 1443 • Newport News, VA 23601 • 757-596-5553
www.HelpHabitatforHumanity.org

Printed in the USA
CPSIA information can be obtained
at www.ICGtesting.com
JSHW052015140824
68134JS00027B/2487